Amazing

STORIES FROM
EXODUS

Group®

Loveland, Colorado

Amazing Stories From Exodus

First Printing, 1994

Contributors
Dave Gallagher, Susan Grover, Cheryl Reames, Cindy Smith

Credits
Edited by Joette Whims
Cover designed and illustrated by Sam Thiewes
Interior designed by Dori Walker
Illustrations by Jeff Carnehl

Library of Congress Cataloging-in-Publication Data
Amazing stories from Exodus / [contributors, Dave Gallagher ... et al.].
            p.   cm.
        ISBN 1-55945-198-X
        1. Bible stories, English--O.T. Exodus. 2. Bible games and puzzles. 3. Bible crafts. [1. Bible stories--O.T. Exodus. 2. Bible games and puzzles. 3. Bible crafts.] I. Gallagher, Dave.
    II. Group Publishing.
    BS551.2.A47 1994
    220.9'505--dc20   94-4981
                                                                        CIP
                                                                        AC

Printed in the United States of America.

CONTENTS

INTRODUCTION

The stories in the book of Exodus show how God used his great power to help the children of Israel. As kids discover how God helped Moses, Aaron, Hur, and others, they'll learn to trust God with their own lives. *Amazing Stories From Exodus* brings these Bible heroes to life for third- and fourth-graders with a fascinating variety of active learning experiences. In each lesson you'll find activities that appeal to every kind of learner and learning style.

Active learning helps students understand the important biblical truths behind each story and discover how those truths apply to their daily lives. You'll enjoy seeing your students' enthusiasm as they get involved in games, simple crafts, skits, group interaction, art projects, and lively stories. And you'll be amazed to see how much kids remember when, instead of just listening, they're given opportunity to *participate*.

With each lesson you'll find the Bible basis, a simple lesson outline for your personal preparation, and a list of easily obtainable supplies. Many lessons contain photocopiable handouts. Lessons range from 45 to 60 minutes, depending on the size of your class and the number of activities you choose.

Amazing Stories From Exodus will bring the Bible to life in your classroom and challenge your students to deepen their relationships with our amazing God.

LESSON 1
GOD'S TREASURES

Story: Baby Moses Is Adopted
Exodus 2:1-10
Good News: God loves his adopted children.

What would you do if a baby you loved was faced with a death sentence? Because the king of Egypt was afraid the enslaved Israelites would mutiny, he issued a command to throw all Hebrew baby boys into the Nile River. After three months, Moses' parents could no longer hide their growing, active baby. They laid him in a basket and placed him along the edge of the Nile River where the king's daughter found him. She was drawn to baby Moses and adopted him as her child.

Just as Moses was adopted, those who accept Jesus as Lord of their lives are adopted into God's family. Romans 8:15b says, "You have received a spirit of adoption as sons by which we cry out, 'Abba! Father!' " (New American Standard Bible). This lesson will help children understand the depth of God's love for them.

A Look at the Lesson

1. A Treasure Hidden (10 minutes)—Kids will find a hidden treasure and tell about things they treasure.

2. A Treasure Found (10 minutes)—Kids will act out the story of baby Moses from Exodus 2:1-10.

3. A Treasure Revealed (7 minutes)—Students will put the words of 1 John 3:1 in order.

4. Discovering Bible Treasures (10 minutes)—Kids will write on hearts ways God shows love and display the hearts on a wall.

5. More Treasure Uncovered (10 minutes)—Students will form links with partners to show how God hangs onto them during difficult situations.

6. Treasure to the Top (10 minutes)—Children will push apples under water to show that God's love always surrounds them.

7. We're a Treasure to God (3 minutes)—Students will stand and hold apples to show that they are the apple of God's eye.

Preparation

Gather Bibles; construction paper in blue, green, and another color; tape; scissors; one quarter; 3×5 cards; a basket or a box; a baby blanket; a small doll; and a larger doll. You'll also need pencils, a photocopy of the "God Loves Me!" handout (p. 13), two buckets of water, apples, and towels.

1 A Treasure Hidden

(You'll need blue and green construction paper, tape, scissors, pencils, and a quarter.)

Give each child one sheet each of blue and green construction paper, tape, scissors, and a pencil.

Say: **Our story today takes place by a river. Let's make a river with tall stalks of grass around it. To make waves in the river, cut your blue construction paper into long, wavy strips.**

Have the children scatter their "blue waves" across one side of the room.

Demonstrate how to make the tall stalks of "grass" by cutting the green paper into ½-inch strips, leaving three inches uncut at the bottom. Show

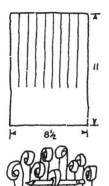

kids how to curl each stalk of grass by rolling it around a pencil. Form a circle with the paper and tape it together at the bottom.

Have the children place their tall grass along the sides of the river. While the children are doing this, hide a quarter somewhere in the tall grass.

Say: **I've hidden a treasure in or near the river. On the count of three, see who can be the first one to find it. Be careful not push or run. Ready? One, two, three!**

After the quarter has been found, ask the kids to straighten the river and reeds for the next activity.

Ask:

● **When I said I had hidden a treasure, what did you think it was?**

● **What are some things people treasure besides money?**

Have kids turn to a partner and tell about two or three of their favorite treasures. Then say: **Today we're going to learn about a very special treasure someone found beside a river back in Bible times.**

2 A Treasure Found

(You'll need Bibles, 3×5 cards, a pencil, the river and grass from the last activity, a basket or a box, a baby blanket, a small doll, and a larger doll. The dolls can be magazine pictures.)

Write the following messages on separate 3×5 cards, then mark them #1, #2, and #3.

1. " 'This is one of the Hebrew babies.' "

2. " 'Take this baby and nurse him for me, and I will pay you.' "

3. " 'Would you like me to go and find a Hebrew woman to nurse the baby for you?' "

Say: **Our story is found in Exodus 2:1-10. First, we'll read it with partners, then I'll read it through again as you act out the story.**

Form pairs and have them scatter around the room. Instruct the kids to turn to Exodus 2 and take turns reading the first 10 verses to each other.

When the kids have finished reading, ask for volunteers to play the parts of Moses' father, his mother, his sister, and the king's daughter. Place some of the kids on their knees among the handmade reeds to sway like gently blowing grass, and let the rest play the role of servant girls. Give the 3×5 cards marked #1 and #2 to the king's daughter and the one marked #3 to Moses' sister.

Say: **As I read the story again, listen for your character. Use your imagination as you act out your part.**

"Now a man from the family of Levi married a woman who was also from the family of Levi." Have Moses' father and mother stand together.

"**She became pregnant and gave birth to a son.**" Hand the smaller doll to Moses' mother.

"**When she saw how wonderful the baby was, she hid him for three months.**

"**But after three months she was not able to hide the baby any longer, so she got a basket and covered it with tar so that it would float. She put the baby in the basket.**" Give Moses' mother the basket or box and the blanket. Have her lay the doll inside and cover it with the blanket.

"**Then she put the basket among the tall stalks of grass at the edge of the Nile River.**

"**The baby's sister stood a short distance away to see what would happen to him.**

"**Then the daughter of the king of Egypt came to the river to take a bath, and her servant girls were walking beside the river.**

"**When she saw the basket in the tall grass, she sent her slave girl to get it.**

"**The king's daughter opened the basket and saw the baby boy.**

"**He was crying, so she felt sorry for him and said...**" Have the daughter read the 3×5 card marked #1.

"**Then the baby's sister asked the king's daughter...**" Have Moses' sister step forward and read her 3×5 card.

"**The king's daughter said, 'Go!' So the girl went and got the baby's own mother.**" Have Moses' sister get her mother and bring her to the king's daughter.

"**The king's daughter said to the woman...**" Have the king's daughter read the card marked #2.

"**So the woman took her baby and nursed him.**

"**When the child grew older, the woman took him to the king's daughter, and she adopted the baby as her own son.**" Exchange the smaller doll for the larger doll and have Moses' mother give it to the king's daughter.

"**The king's daughter named him Moses [meaning 'to draw out'], because she had pulled him out of the water.**"

Compliment the children and thank them for their participation.

Ask:

● **Why would it be hard to keep a baby hidden?**

● **How do you think the king's daughter felt when she saw what was in the basket?**

● **Why do you think she wanted the baby?**

● **Since the king's daughter adopted baby Moses, whose family did Moses become a part of?**

If some children in your class are adopted, be sensitive to their feelings about adoption. If they are comfortable talking about it, encourage them to be the "experts" in your discussion. If they feel awkward or hesitant to talk about their adoption, don't put them on the spot.

Ask a volunteer to read Psalm 5:2.

Say: **The Bible says God is King. When we decide to follow Jesus, God adopts us into his family. Just like baby Moses, we become a King's kid! When a child is adopted into a family, the parents love that child as if he or she had been born to them. God is the same way. Let's uncover more about this special treasure of God's love for us.**

3 A Treasure Revealed

(You'll need construction paper, scissors, and a pencil.)

Before class, cut 14 heart shapes from construction paper. On each heart write one word of the following verse: "The Father has loved us so much that we are called children of God" (1 John 3:1). Number the words in correct sequence. For example, print "The" on one heart and "1" either above or below it, print "Father" and "2" on another heart, and so on.

If you have more than 14 students, cut the hearts out in two different colors and make two sets of verses. Have the class form two groups. Give one group one color of hearts and the second group the other color.

Give each child a heart. It's OK if some children get more than one heart.

Say: **Stand in a line according to where your number fits.**

When the kids are in the right order, have them each say their word aloud one at a time to complete the sentence. Do this several times. Then ask a volunteer to repeat the verse.

Say: **Since we are adopted sons and daughters, God has included us in his family. We can call him our Father. We can be sure he loves us like a father.** Ask:

● **How does that make you feel?**

● **What do you think you might do differently because you know how much God loves you?**

Say: **Let's think about some ways God shows his love to us.**

4 Discovering Bible Treasures

(You'll need Bibles, hearts from the last activity, pencils, scissors, and tape. You will also need a photocopy of the "God Loves Me!" handout. If you have more than 12 children in your class, make two copies of the handout. Cut the verses apart.)

Ask:

● **How do your parents show that they love you?**

Say: **Well, we can't physically feel God hugging us. And we can't see him when he talks to us. But God does show us in many ways how much he loves us. Let's find out what some of those ways are.**

Hand each child a pencil and one of the Scripture references from the "God Loves Me!" handout. It's OK if more than one person receives the same reference.

Say: **Look up and read your Bible verse. Then write on the back of your construction paper heart what that verse says about how God shows he loves us.**

Have the kids tell the class what they discovered in their verses, then say: **Below what you wrote about God's love, write down one specific way God has shown love to you. For instance, you could write, "He gives me food," or "He helped me on my math test this week."**

When the children have finished, arrange their hearts in a heart shape on the wall. For an added bonus, take an instant-print picture of the class and put it inside the heart shape.

Say: **There's another important thing we need to know about God's love.**

5 More Treasure Uncovered

(You will need Bibles.)

Have kids form trios. Put boys with boys and girls with girls. Instruct two people in each group to stand back to back and link arms.

If your class is not evenly divisible by three, form one or two groups of four and have kids change roles so that everyone has a chance to participate.

Say: **The person who is not linked is to try to pull the other two**

kids apart. **Let's see if it can be done.**

Call for time after a few moments and have kids change places in their trios. Then have kids exchange places one more time so that everyone has a chance at each position.

Call time again. Gather everyone together and ask:

● **Why couldn't you pull your friends apart?**

Ask for volunteers to read Romans 8:35 and 38-39.

● **Have you ever been through a tough time when you wondered if God really loved you? Explain.**

● **What are some other troubling situations that might cause us to wonder about God's love for us?**

● **How was what your partner did when someone was trying to pull you apart like what God does when we're facing a tough time?**

Ask another volunteer to read Psalm 34:18.

Say: **God hangs on to us even tighter when we're hurting. The Bible says absolutely nothing can separate us from God's love. He always surrounds us with love. To show how we can be like God, let's give each other a hug.**

Gather children in a circle and have them hug each other.

6 Treasure to the Top

(You'll need a Bible, two buckets filled with water, apples, and a couple of small towels.)

Give each child an apple and invite the kids to kneel around the water buckets. Have the children push their sleeves up above their elbows.

Say: **Pretend that your feelings are like the apple. Push your apples down to the bottom and hold them there.**

Ask:

● **How do you feel after you've done something wrong?**

Say: **When we do wrong things, we feel bad. Sometimes we feel weighted down. Our hearts are heavy. We feel like no one loves us anymore, not even God. We think we've let God down.**

Ask:

● **How do you feel when something bad happens to you?**

Say: **Sometimes problems and difficult situations can also make us fell weighted down. We begin wondering if God cares about us. But we just learned that *nothing* can separate us from God's love, not even when we do wrong things, not even when something hurts us.** Ask:

● **How is the water in this bucket like God's love?**

● When you pushed your apple to the bottom, was it surrounded by less water? Why not?

● How do you feel after you've asked God to forgive you?

● How do you feel when problems are solved?

Say: **Gently let your apple come to the top.** Pass the towels around as you continue with the lesson.

● **What brought your apple back to the top?**

● **How is this like what happens when you know God has forgiven you or helped you in a difficult situation?**

Ask a volunteer to read Romans 8:37.

Say: **We'll all face trouble in our lives. But the Bible says we'll be victorious because God's love surrounds us. God will help us rise to the top!**

7 We're a Treasure to God

Have the kids stand in a circle and hold their apples.

Say: **In the Bible, God calls us the apple of his eye. That means we are very special to him. Since we are God's adopted children, we are his treasures. He loves us very much. Take your apple home. When you eat it, remember that you have a heavenly Father who loves you dearly.**

GOD LOVES ME!

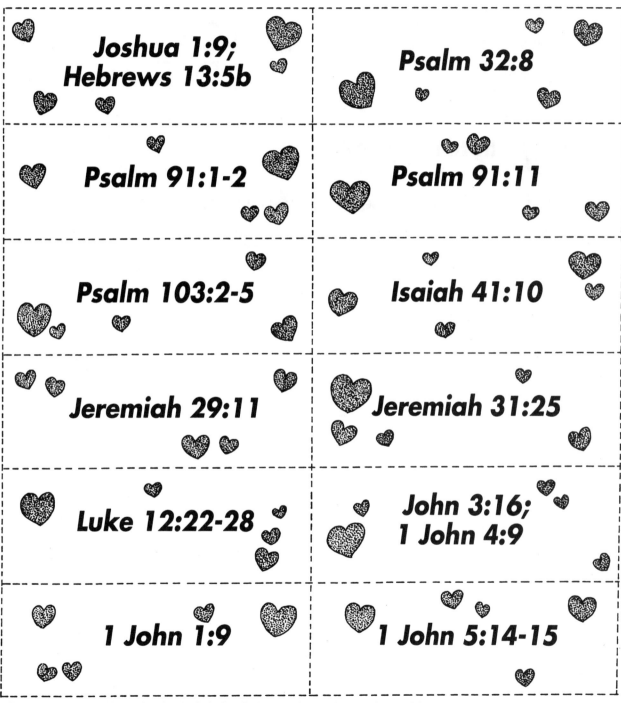

**Joshua 1:9;
Hebrews 13:5b**

Psalm 32:8

Psalm 91:1-2

Psalm 91:11

Psalm 103:2-5

Isaiah 41:10

Jeremiah 29:11

Jeremiah 31:25

Luke 12:22-28

**John 3:16;
1 John 4:9**

1 John 1:9

1 John 5:14-15

LESSON 2

YOU CAN DO IT!

Story: The Burning Bush
Exodus 3:1–4:20

Good News: Because God will help us accomplish hard tasks, we can have confidence in our abilities.

When God asked Moses to deliver the people of Israel from captivity in Egypt, Moses argued that he couldn't do the job. Even when God said he would help Moses with the task and that the outcome was certain, Moses continued to insist that he couldn't do what God required.

Moses, like many of us, lacked confidence in his abilities to accomplish the task God set before him. God had to reassure Moses that he could indeed do the job and that God would provide the assistance Moses needed. This lesson will help kids understand that they have unrecognized strengths and that God will help them accomplish hard tasks.

A Look at the Lesson

1. Impossible Tasks (8 minutes)—Students will talk with their mouths taped half-shut and discuss how they respond to difficult tasks.
2. Great Excuses (10 minutes)—Kids will write excuses they make.
3. Excuses Around the Burning Bush (10 minutes)—Kids will tear out bushes and flames from paper and guess the excuses Moses made.
4. Answers to Excuses (12 minutes)—Students will write God's answers to Moses' excuses and tell how the answers can make them more confident.
5. Hidden Strengths (15 minutes)—Students will make paper-plate barbells to remind them how they can use their strengths in hard situations.
6. Our Heavenly Helper (5 minutes)—Kids will thank God for their strengths.

Preparation

Gather Bibles; masking tape; newsprint; markers; 8½ × 11-inch sheets of green construction paper; 5½ × 2-inch strips of red construction paper; pencils; glue or glue sticks; slips of paper; drinking straws; and, for each student, two small paper plates.

1 Impossible Tasks

(You'll need masking tape.)

Give children masking tape and ask them to tape one side of their mouths shut. Say: **I'm going to give you 10 seconds to think of a joke. I will tell you when the time is up.**

After 10 seconds have passed, say: **With one-half of your mouth taped, tell your joke to two or three people.**

Give kids a minute or two to talk to others. Then have them remove the tape from their mouths and throw it away. Ask:

● **What was it like to think of a joke so quickly?**
● **What was it like to tell your joke with half your mouth taped shut?**
● **What do you do when you're asked to do tasks that seem impossible?**

Say: **Sometimes we try to talk our way out of hard jobs. We might make excuses like "I could never do that" or "I don't know what to** say." Let's think about excuses we make to avoid doing things that we feel are too difficult.

2 Great Excuses

(You'll need three sheets of newsprint and markers.)

Ask students to think about excuses they've made to avoid doing difficult tasks. For example, they might say, "My family is having company, so I can't," "I have a sore toe," or "I just don't want to."

Form three teams and give each team a sheet of newsprint and some markers. Ask teams to write as many excuses on their newsprint as they can in two minutes.

After two minutes, call time. Ask a volunteer from each group to read the group's excuses aloud. Then ask:

● **Why do people make excuses?**

● **Who can tell about a time when you made an excuse to get out of doing something that seemed difficult?**

If kids hesitate to share, encourage them by telling about an excuse you made to avoid something difficult.

Say: **Did you know that even people we think of as Bible heroes sometimes made excuses? Today we're going to find out about a time when God asked Moses to do something hard. Guess what Moses did—he made excuses.**

3 Excuses Around the Burning Bush

(You'll need Bibles, 8½ × 11-inch sheets of green construction paper, 5½ × 2-inch strips of red construction paper, pencils, and glue or glue sticks.)

Say: **One day Moses was taking care of some sheep when he saw a very strange sight. Let's open our Bibles to Exodus 3 and find out what he saw.**

Help children find Exodus 3 and ask a volunteer to read verses 1-6 aloud. Give each student a sheet of green construction paper, three 5½ × 2-inch strips of red construction paper, and a pencil. Have kids tear their green paper into the shape of a bush and tear one large flame from each slip of red paper.

Say: **Moses was afraid when he heard God speaking from the burning bush. Moses became more afraid when he found out what God wanted, so he started making excuses. In the story we'll discover what some of those excuses were. When we get to certain places in the story, we'll stop and you can guess what Moses said to God. Write your guess on one of your red flames.**

Say: **First, let's read about the hard task God wanted Moses to do.** Ask volunteers to read verse 7 and verses 9-10. Say: **What excuse do you think Moses gave?** Pause to let kids each write an excuse on one of their flames. Invite volunteers to share their excuses. Then ask a volunteer to read Exodus 3:11 aloud.

Say: **Moses didn't think he could do what God asked. God said to Moses, "I will be with you." But Moses still didn't think he could do what God asked. Moses said that the people would wonder who sent him and that he didn't know what to tell them. Then God showed Moses two miracles he would perform to help the people accept him as their leader. But Moses still tried to make excuses. He was afraid people wouldn't believe him. Let's see what God told Moses to do.** Have a volunteer read Exodus 4:8-9.

Say: **Moses still didn't have confidence that he could do what God asked. Moses thought he had a problem that would keep him from doing a good job. He used his problem as another excuse. What do you think his problem was?** Have kids each write an excuse on their second flame. Let some of the kids share their excuses. Then have a student read Exodus 4:10 aloud.

Say: **God promised to help Moses speak. Moses was running out of excuses. What do you think he finally said to God?** Have the children each write another guess on their third flame. Allow several children to share their ideas. Then ask a volunteer to read Exodus 4:13.

Say: **Moses asked God to send someone in his place. Moses had a hard time believing that God could help him lead the people.**

Have the kids glue their flames to the tops of their bushes with the excuses showing on the back sides. Using glue sticks rather than liquid glue will keep the bushes from getting wet. This will help during the next activity when the children will write on their bushes.

Say: **We found out what excuses Moses gave to get out of his difficult task. But God had answers for every excuse. God would provide the strength and help Moses needed. Now let's look at what God said to answer Moses' excuses and give him the confidence he needed.**

Answers to Excuses

(You'll need Bibles, slips of paper, the burning bushes made in the previous activity, and pencils.)

Say: **God had an answer for each of Moses' excuses.**

Have kids return to the three teams formed earlier. Write each of the following excuses and Bible passages on a separate piece of paper. Give each team one of these slips of paper.

"Who, me?"—Exodus 3:11-12

"I can't talk well."—Exodus 4:10-12

"Ask somebody else."—Exodus 4:13-16

Say: **Have one person read your passage aloud. When you've found Moses' excuse, write it on the back of your bush. When you find God's answer, write it on the front of your bush.**

Give kids about three minutes to work. Then call everyone together and invite representatives from each group to share the excuses and responses. Then ask:

● **What did God promise to help Moses feel more confident?**

● **How do you feel about what God said to Moses?**

● **What do you think God might say to us when we think we can't do something?**

Say: **Let's learn a Bible verse that can help us remember that God can make us strong.** Help kids look up Exodus 15:2 and read it aloud together. Ask:

● **What's something hard you have to do this week?**

● **How can this verse or the sentence you wrote on your bush help you be more confident in this situation?**

Say: **Moses was afraid he couldn't do what God asked. But God knew what Moses could do. God gave Moses all the help he needed to do the job.**

Hidden Strengths

(You'll need two small paper plates for each child, pencils, and drinking straws.)

Say: **Sometimes we're like Moses. We think about what we *can't* do instead of thinking about what we *can* do with God's help. But sometimes other people see strengths in us that we may not know we have.**

Have kids sit in a circle. Give each child two paper plates. Tell them to write their names on both plates.

Have kids pass their plates around the circle in different directions at the same time.

Say: **When each plate comes to you, read the name and write down a strength that person has. For example, you could write, "good listener," "sense of humor," "strong handshake," or "many friends."**

Children may be tempted to write negative comments on the plates. Tell them to write only positive things about one another. Explain that we can find good things about everyone, even people we don't know well or have trouble getting along with sometimes. Practicing saying good things helps us to see the good in others.

After the plates have gone halfway around the circle, have kids pass them back to their owners. Give kids a moment to read what's on their plates, then ask:

● **What went through your mind when you saw what others had written about you?**

● **How can this list help when you face a hard task?**

Say: **Let's use these plates to make something that will help us remember our strengths.**

Give each child a drinking straw. Have children use pencils to punch a hole in the center of each plate. Have them put a plate on each end of the drinking straw to make barbells. Explain that the barbells will remind them of their recognized and hidden strengths.

Say: **Sometimes it's surprising to discover the strengths we have within us. God sees even more strengths in each of us. Other people may see those strengths, too. Let's praise God for the help he gives us to use those strengths when we may be afraid to try.**

6 Our Heavenly Helper

(You'll need everyone's burning bushes and barbells.)

Have the children sit in a circle on the floor. Tell them to place their burning bushes in front of them with the "answer" sides up and to put the barbells on them. Close by praying a prayer similar to this one: **Dear God, thank you for giving us the help we need to do hard tasks. Thank you for seeing strengths in us we may not know we have. Help us discover those strengths as we try to do what you want us to do. Amen.**

LESSON 3
SAYING GOOD WORDS

Story: The People Complain, Then Moses Complains

Exodus 5:1–6:13

Good News: Positive, encouraging words are contagious.

When Moses and Aaron asked the king of Egypt to let the Israelites go, the king made it more difficult for the Israelites to meet their work quota. He made their work environment almost unbearable. The children of Israel complained to Moses who, in turn, complained to God. God replied with a promise of freedom for his people. Yet the Israelites were too discouraged to listen to God's reply. As a result, Moses became disheartened and complained again when God told him to return to Pharaoh.

Complaining is no less a problem today than in Moses' time. When we become dissatisfied, our natural tendency is to grumble. James 3:2 says if we can learn to control our tongue, we can control our whole body. This lesson will help kids understand that complaining fosters a hostile atmosphere, but encouraging, positive words help create a loving, hopeful environment.

A Look at the Lesson

1. Flying Paper Balls (10 minutes)—Kids will toss paper balls to learn how contagious complaining is.

2. Smile or Frown (10 minutes)—Students will listen to the Bible story, smile at encouraging words, and frown at a whining voice.

3. Down the Hatch (6 minutes)—Children will eat wrapped candies and look up Philippians 2:14.

4. Encouraging Words (12 minutes)—Students will look up Bible verses and choose appropriate positive words for difficult situations.

5. Smiles (10 minutes)—Children will play a game of Smilers and Grumps.

6. A Paper Mouth (12 minutes)—Kids will make paper mouths, listen to Philippians 2:14, and practice using positive words.

Preparation

Gather Bibles, scrap paper, and wrapped candy such as chocolate kisses. You'll also need a photocopy of the "What You Could Say Instead Is..." handout (p. 26), scissors, 8½ × 11 sheets of white paper, markers, slips of paper, pencils, and glue.

1 Flying Paper Balls

(You'll need pieces of scrap paper.)

Have kids sit in a circle. Lay several pieces of scrap paper in front of each child and keep some for yourself. Begin wadding up your pieces into balls and throwing them at the students to initiate a paper-ball fight. Encourage students to get involved by saying: **I bet you can't hit me.**

After about 30 seconds of paper-ball throwing, call time. Gather all the paper balls in front of you, then ask:

● **What did you do when I threw paper balls at you?**

● **How is what happened with the paper balls like what happens when people complain?**

● **Who can tell about a time when one person complained, then other people started complaining, too? What happened?**

Say: **Complaining is contagious. When someone in a group begins to complain, it doesn't take long for other people to begin complaining, too. Complaining puts everyone in a bad mood. It's no fun to hear people complain.**

Now, help me pick up these paper balls and throw them away—without complaining!

2 Smile or Frown

Say: **Find a partner and sit facing each other. As I tell the story, smile at your partner when someone in the story speaks encouraging words and frown when someone complains.**

Read the following story based on Exodus 5:1–6:13. Use a bright, happy voice when you read encouraging words and a whining voice when you read complaints.

Say: **The Egyptians had forced the Israelites to become their slaves. God saw how hard they had to work, so God chose Moses to do a very important job. God said:** (happy voice) **"Moses, I am sending you to the king of Egypt. I want you to bring my people, the Israelites, out of Egypt!" But when Moses asked the king to let God's people go, the king became angry and made them work even harder!**

The Israelites came to Moses and complained: (whine) **"You've caused the king and his officers to hate us. We can't keep up with all this work. You've given them an excuse to kill us!"**

Moses went back to God and complained: (whine) **"Lord, why have you brought this trouble on your people? Is this why you sent me here?"**

God heard Moses' complaint. He said to Moses: (happy voice) **"Now you will see what I will do for my people. I will use my great power against the king, and he will let my people go. Because of my power, the king will want my people out of his country."**

Moses was so excited about God's promise that he went straight to the Israelites and said, (happy voice) **"God told me he's going to set you free!"**

But God's people still grumbled. They didn't want to listen to Moses. They complained: (whine) **"Moses, we don't believe you. Our work has just gotten harder since you showed up!"**

Then God said to Moses, "Go back to the king of Egypt and tell him one more time to let my people go."

Moses complained: (whine) **"If the Israelites won't listen to me, I'm sure the king won't listen to me either. I'm not good at talking to people."**

Then God told Moses once more to lead the Israelites out of Egypt. Ask:

● **Why did the Israelites complain to Moses?**
● **Why did Moses complain to God?**
● **What happens when people start complaining?**

Say: **When we complain, frowns suddenly appear on everyone's face. Other bad things happen, too.**

3 ▷ Down the Hatch

(You'll need Bibles and wrapped candies such as chocolate kisses.)

Have kids sit in a circle on the floor. Give each child a small handful of candies.

Say: **Give one piece of candy to the person on your right and say sweet words about that person. For example, you could say, "I like the way you smile" or "You have a kind way of talking to people."**

Give kids a moment to compliment each other.

Say: **Now give a candy to the person on your left and say sweet words about that person.**

After the children have complimented one another and eaten their candies, ask:

● **What was it like to give away candy and encouraging words?**
● **How are encouraging words like candy?**
● **What happens when people start to encourage one another instead of complaining?**

Say: **Listen to what the Bible says about complaining.**

Have the children look up Philippians 2:14. Have a volunteer read it aloud. Then ask:

● **What would happen if we chose to say encouraging words when we felt like complaining?**

Say: **Let's practice saying encouraging words right now.**

4 ▷ Encouraging Words

(You'll need Bibles, a photocopy of the "What You Could Say Instead Is…" handout, and scissors. Cut the handout apart on the dotted lines.)

Form trios. Give each group one of the complaints. It's OK if more than one group has the same situation.

Say: **Moses complained even though God promised to set the peo-**

ple free. Instead of complaining, Moses could have said encouraging words like "God said the Israelites will be freed. I believe it. I won't complain. I'll trust God to do what he says he will do." Someone is complaining in each of the situations I've given you. Read the paragraph, look up the verse, then decide what positive words you could say instead.

Allow two or three minutes for groups to read their situations aloud and think of encouraging words. Then gather kids together and have a volunteer from each group read the group's situation and share its encouraging words.

Say: **We can choose the kind of words that come out of our mouths. The next time you feel like complaining, remember how good it makes everyone feel when you speak positive words instead.**

5 Smiles

Form two groups. Have the groups sit in straight lines facing each other. Designate one group as the smilers and the other as the grumps.

Say: **I want all the smilers to smile as big as you can at the grumps and the grumps to avoid smiling. Smilers, your job is to make the grumps smile. As soon as someone on the grump team smiles, that person has to stand up.**

Wait until most of the grumps are standing, then ask:

● **Those of you on the grump team, what made you smile?**

● **Those of you on the smiling team, how did it make you feel to make someone smile?**

Say: **We found out earlier that complaining is contagious. Well, so are positive words. When we speak good words, we're encouraged and those around us are encouraged. We bring smiles to people's faces. Let's smile as we pray.**

Father, help us not to grumble or complain. Thank you for the Bible which gives us your sweet words to say. Help us encourage people with our positive words. Amen.

6 A Paper Mouth

(You'll need a Bible, 8½×11 sheets of paper, markers, slips of paper small enough to fit inside the handmade mouths, pencils, and glue.)

Say: **We're going to make mouths from paper to help us remember not to complain.**

Hand out paper and markers. Using the directions below, demonstrate each step as the students follow along. Let the children draw eyes and color the lips. Give each child a small slip of paper and a pencil. Ask a volunteer to read Philippians 2:14.

Say: **On your slip of paper write, "I will not complain about..."** **Finish the sentence with a complaint you often say. For instance, you could write, "I will not complain about washing the dishes." Then glue your slip of paper on the back of your paper mouth so your sentence can be seen from the front. When you finish, repeat your sentence to a partner by "talking" with your paper mouth. Then use your mouth to say sweet words about what you wrote. You might say, "I'm so glad I can help mother with dishes because she does so much for me."**

As the children leave, invite them to keep their paper mouths in their rooms to remind them to say encouraging words.

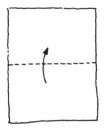

1. Fold a sheet of paper in half.

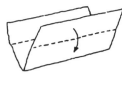

2. Fold the top edge to the middle.

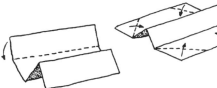

3. Fold the bottom edge to the middle.

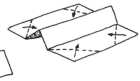

4. Turn the paper over. Fold each corner back to make a triangle.

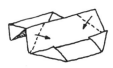

5. Fold down the two top corners.

6. Fold both sides up.

7. Turn over. Tear a small slit in the middle of the two long edges.

8. Fold the torn edges down on each side.

9. Spread apart.

10. Squeeze together at arrows. Color lips and draw eyes.

What you could say instead is...

I hate the way I look today. Yuk!

Read Psalm 139:14, then change the complaining words to encouraging words.

What you could say instead is...

Math is too hard for me. I just don't understand it. I'm never going to understand it.

Read Philippians 4:13, then change the complaining words to encouraging words.

What you could say instead is...

My parents are moving right in the middle of the school year. I don't want to go! I'll have to start all over again. What if no one likes me in this new school?

Read Joshua 1:9, then change the complaining words to encouraging words.

What you could say instead is...

I always have to watch my baby brother while Mom fixes dinner. Sometimes he can be a real pain! I wish I didn't have a little brother!

Read 1 John 4:7, then change the complaining words to encouraging words.

LESSON 4
IT'S GOOD TO LISTEN

Story: God's Warning and the Plagues
Exodus 7:1-6; 7:13–10:29
Good News: God rewards those who listen and respond to God's message.

*T*he people of Israel asked to be free so they could worship and serve God. But the king of Egypt refused to listen to Moses' pleas and God's warnings to release the people. Because of this, God promised to do many miracles in Egypt so the people would recognize God's power and obey God's message.

Moses and the people of Israel received rewards for listening to God. The king and the people of Egypt suffered greatly because they refused to listen to God. This lesson will help kids understand that God rewards those who listen and respond to God's message.

A Look at the Lesson

1. Listener Simon Says (12 minutes)—Children will play Listener Simon Says to learn the importance of listening.

2. Biting Flies (12 minutes)—Kids will use stick-on dots to represent fly bites, listen to parts of Exodus 8, and find out what happened when the king didn't listen to God.

3. Total Darkness (10 minutes) Kids will put on blindfolds, listen to Exodus 10:21-27, and discuss what can happen when we don't listen to God.

4. Happy Listeners (8 minutes)—Students will play a whisper game, read Luke 11:28, and discover what happens when we listen to God.

5. Listening Ears (12 minutes)—Kids will make big ears and say good things to one another.

6. Other Ways to Communicate (6 minutes)—Students will act out ways to communicate and thank God for giving them ways to listen.

Preparation

Gather Bibles, cotton balls, bite-sized fruit snacks, small stick-on dots, blindfolds, and 3×3-inch squares of black construction paper. You'll also need photocopies of the "Big Ears" handout (p. 34), scissors, glue, and poster board or heavy paper.

1 Listener Simon Says

(You'll need cotton balls and bite-sized fruit snacks.)

Gather the class into a semicircle and have kids number off by twos. Say: **Today we're playing Listener Simon Says. All the ones will be listeners. All the twos will be nonlisteners. Listeners, do whatever I say when I begin Simon Says. Nonlisteners, don't follow any directions. I'll give you cotton balls to put in your ears to help you ignore what I say.**

Have the nonlisteners gently put cotton balls into their ears and put their hands over their ears. Play the game and reward the listeners with fruit snacks every time they follow the directions correctly. After a few commands, have the listeners and nonlisteners change roles. Have nonlisteners take out the cotton balls and discard them and give the listeners new cotton balls to put in their ears. Give a few more commands. Then have students remove and discard the used cotton balls.

Have everyone sit down, then ask:

● **Who got treats? Why?**

● **Why did I reward only the listeners who followed my directions correctly?**

● **How is this like what happens to you at school or at home when you listen or don't listen?**

● **What are some consequences that can happen when people refuse to listen to an important message?**

Say: **It may seem fun to refuse to listen and do whatever we want, but sometimes there are rewards for listening and negative consequences for not listening. Today we're going to learn what happened in the Bible when some people listened to God and did what God said and what happened to others who didn't listen.**

2 Biting Flies

(You'll need Bibles and small stick-on dots.)

Say: **God told Moses to rescue the people of Israel from the king of Egypt. To get the Israelites out of Egypt, God sent many messages to the king and his people. But the king was stubborn. He refused to listen to God. God wanted everyone to know how important it is to listen to God and follow his instructions. So God had Moses do some miracles to make the king listen.**

Distribute 10 stick-on dots to each person.

Say: **Imagine that you didn't listen to a message. Because you refused to listen, you are bitten by flies. These stick-on dots are fly bites. But flies can only bite nonlisteners. Listeners can't be bitten.**

Designate two people as listeners who can't receive fly bites. Let kids, including the listeners, pretend to be flies that "bite" by putting the stick-on dots on other people. Let kids have fun with this but encourage them not to get rough. After kids stick on all the fly bites, gather everyone together. Ask:

● **What was it like to be "stuck" with a fly bite?**

● **What do you think you would do if those dots really were stinging fly bites?**

● **How did you feel about the listeners who didn't get bitten?**

Say: **This is like something that happened to the people in Egypt. Let's look at Exodus 8 to find out what happened.**

Help kids locate Exodus 8. Have a volunteer read Exodus 8:20-23 aloud. Ask:

● **Would you listen to a warning like this? Why or why not?**

Say: **Let's read some more and find out whether the king listened and obeyed God.**

Have volunteers read two verses each from Exodus 8:24-32. Ask:

● **Why do you think God sent flies to bite the king and his people?**

● **What do you suppose the king and his people thought when the flies bit them and didn't bite Moses and the people of Israel?**

● **If you were the king, would you listen to God the next time? Why or why not?**

Say: **After the flies went away, the king changed his mind again. He refused to let the people go.**

3 Total Darkness

(You'll need a Bible, blindfolds, and 3×3-inch squares of black construction paper.)

Say: **When the king still didn't listen, God sent other consequences. Let's see what happened when the king still refused to listen to God.**

Hand out squares of black construction paper and blindfolds to the children. Form pairs and have partners help each other gently place the squares of paper over their eyes, then tie on the blindfolds. When everyone is blindfolded, give this series of commands:

● **Hold hands with your partner.**

● **Walk to the door.**

● **Walk to the table.**

● **Find another pair of students and shake hands with them.**

● **Find chairs and sit down.**

While kids are still blindfolded, ask:

● **How would you handle it if you had to live in complete darkness for three days?**

● **How would you get food?**

● **What would be especially hard to do?**

● **After spending three days in darkness, what would you be thinking?**

Say: **While you still have your blindfolds on, let me tell you what happened to the king when he didn't listen to God.**

Read or tell Exodus 10:21-27. Ask:

● **Why do you think God sent darkness?**

● **How is this experience like what can happen when we don't listen to God?**

Have the children take off their blindfolds.

Say: **God used the plagues of flies and darkness to let the Egyptian and Israelite people know that it's important to listen to and follow God's instructions.**

4 Happy Listeners

(You'll need Bibles.)

Sit in a circle.

Say: **We just learned how important it is to listen, especially to God. Now let's see how well you can listen. I'm going to whisper something to one person, then that person will whisper to someone else.**

Whisper into one person's ear: **People who listen to and obey God are happy.** After the message has been passed around, ask the last person to repeat what was heard. Ask:

● **What happened to the message? Why?**

Say: **Sometimes we hear God's message clearly and don't pay attention to it. Other times we don't hear God's message clearly, so we don't follow the directions.** Ask:

● **How can we listen to messages from God?**
● **When are good times to listen to God?**
● **What can happen when we don't listen to God?**

Form pairs, then say: **Tell your partner about a time you listened to and followed God's message. For example, you might have remembered that God wants us to obey our parents and followed your parents' instructions at an important time. Then tell a time when you didn't listen or didn't follow God's message. For example, you might have forgotten that God tells us to respect our leaders, ignored your teacher's directions, and failed a test.**

Help children look up Luke 11:28. Have them read the verse aloud with their partners. Ask:

● **What does this verse say to you?**

Say: **When we get a message from God, it's good for us to listen to and obey God.**

5 Listening Ears

(You'll need photocopies of the "Big Ears" handout, scissors, glue, and poster board or heavy paper.)

Distribute photocopies of the "Big Ears" handout, glue, scissors, and poster board or heavy paper. Have kids glue ears onto the poster board and cut out the ears and holes. Have kids each put a big ear over one of their own ears.

Say: **It's important to listen to God. It's also important to listen to others. Sometimes people say good things about us, but we don't listen or pay attention. It's good to listen to the good messages our parents, teachers, and friends say about us. Go to your partner from the last activity. Quietly say something good about that person through the big ear. Then let your partner say something good to you. You might say, "I'm glad you're in our group" or "You're a good listener" or "You have a good sense of humor."**

Allow a minute or two for kids to talk into the big ears. Then gather kids in a circle. Ask:

● **How does it feel to listen to people who are saying good things about you?**

● **Do you think it's important to say good things to others? Why or why not?**

Say: **We all like to hear good things people say to us and about us. God wants us to listen to those things, too.**

6 Other Ways to Communicate

(You'll need the big ears the kids made.)

Say: **We get messages in other ways besides listening with our ears. With your partner, think of one other way you might get a message. When I ask, you and your partner can act out the way to communicate that you chose. For example, you can get messages through your eyes, by hand gestures, or by touch.**

Have children share ideas and plan how to act them out. Then ask volunteers to pantomime their ideas. Let the other kids guess the ideas.

Say: **Let's thank God that we can listen to what God says and that we can listen to one another.**

Have kids sit in a circle and put their big ears in front of them on the floor. Lead a prayer similar to this: **Dear God, we thank you that you have given us ways to listen to you. Help us listen well and do what you want us to do. Thank you for giving us ways to listen to one another. Amen.**

BIG EARS

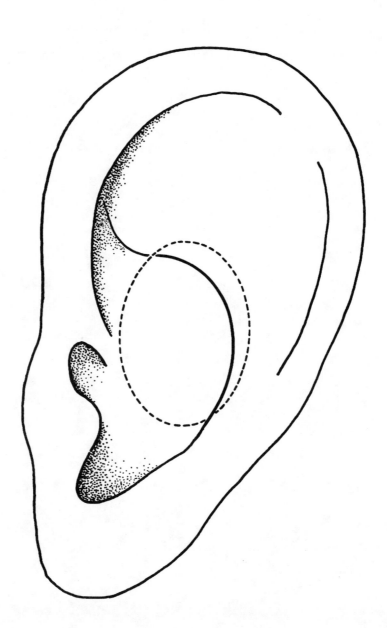

LESSON 5
PROTECTED BY GOD

Story: The First Passover
Exodus 11:1–12:30

Good News: Because God loves us, God protects us.

Because the king of Egypt had hardened his heart and refused to heed the warnings of nine plagues, God sent one more plague on the Egyptian people—the death of the firstborn, both of people and of animals. But while this terrible judgment took place, God provided protection from death for the Israelites. Through Moses, God gave instructions for the Israelites to smear the blood of lambs on their doorposts—a foreshadowing of the sacrifice Jesus would make by shedding his blood to save those who believe and obey. In remembrance of God's mighty acts and protection, God instructed the people to observe the first Passover or Feast of Unleavened Bread.

The story of the death of the firstborn and the first Passover shows that God protects those who love and obey him. This lesson will help kids understand that God wants to be their protector.

A Look at the Lesson

1. Flash of Danger (10 minutes)—Kids will play a game and talk about how it feels to be in danger.

2. Things That Protect (10 minutes)—Students will see common items used for protection and discuss ways they need protection.

3. God Passes Over (15 minutes)—Children will read about the plague of death, read verses from Exodus 11 and 12, and find out how God protected his people.

4. Always Remember (8 minutes)—Students will eat crackers or matzos, listen to Exodus 12:8-17, and learn how God's people remembered God's protection.

5. Protection Prayer (7 minutes)—Children will listen to Psalm 121:5-6 and ask God for his protection.

6. Recalling God's Protection (10 minutes)—Kids will tell specific ways God has protected them and make necklaces to remind them of God's protection.

Preparation

Gather Bibles; a flashlight; masking tape; and items that provide protection, such as potholders, sun lotion, toothpaste, keys, an umbrella, a catcher's mitt, and a hat. You'll also need a bookmark, tape, newsprint, markers, containers of red paint, branches of a shrub to use as brushes, crackers or matzos, cups of water, Life Savers candy, twine, and scissors.

1 Flash of Danger

(You'll need a flashlight and masking tape.)

Create an open space by moving the table and chairs to one side of your classroom. In one corner, mark off a box on the floor with masking tape. Make the box big enough for all the children to stand in it at once. Have kids stand in the opposite corner.

Say: **The light from this flashlight will represent danger. Think of it as a laser. I'll shine it around the room. If the "laser beam" shines on you, drop down and lie flat on the floor. When you're no longer in the light, you can get up and crawl again. Crawl to this box on the floor. When you get inside the box, you are protected from the laser** beam, and you may stand up again.

Turn off the lights. Shine the flashlight around the room until all the kids have made it across the room and are standing inside the box. Turn the lights back on. Have the kids sit in a circle on the floor. Then ask:

- **What was it like to pretend you were in danger?**
- **How did you feel when you got to the safe place?**
- **What kinds of danger do people face today?**
- **What kind of danger is most frightening to you?**
- **What are some things you've learned to do when you're in danger?**

Say: **Today we're going to find out about a whole country that was in danger. Some of the people found God's protection—but others didn't.**

2 Things That Protect

(You'll need a Bible with a bookmark at Exodus 11 and items that provide protection, such as potholders, sun lotion, toothpaste, keys, an umbrella, a catcher's mitt, or a hat. You'll need enough items for each student to have at least one object.)

Place all the items that provide protection in a pile on the floor. Have kids stand in a circle around the pile. One by one, allow kids to choose an object from the pile. Encourage kids to examine their objects carefully. Then ask:

- **Who can tell me what all these things have in common? Explain.**
- **How does each thing provide protection?**
- **What could happen if you didn't have that item?**
- **Which item is most important to you? Explain.**
- **What other things protect you every day?**

Set out a Bible with a bookmark at Exodus 11. Say: **These items protect us from rain and heat and cold. But we can't count on them to protect us from big things. There is someone we can count on, though—God! Today's Bible story is about a time God saved his people from grave danger. Let's find out what happened.**

(You'll need Bibles, tape, two large pieces of newsprint, markers, containers of red watercolors or tempera paint, and small branches of a shrub to use as brushes.)

Say: **Moses tried many ways to convince the king of Egypt to free the people of Israel so they could worship God.** Ask:

● **Who can name some of the things Moses tried?**

Say: **But the king still refused. So God planned a way to make the king and his people willing to let the Israelites go. Let's see what God planned.**

Help children find Exodus 11. Ask a volunteer to read Exodus 11:4-8.

Say: **God knew that the king of Egypt was stubborn. Can you show me what a stubborn king might look like?** (Pause.) **Ooo—you're a pretty scary-looking bunch. This king was scary, too. He was so mean and stubborn that God planned something terrible to make him let the Israelites go: The first son of every household in Egypt would die. But God wanted to protect the people of Israel from death. So God gave Moses a plan. Let's read about that plan.**

Have a volunteer read Exodus 12:21-23.

Say: **God's people painted the door frames of their houses with lambs' blood. This showed that they loved and obeyed God. Let's paint a door frame like the people of Israel did.**

Tape two pieces of newsprint on a wall or door frame. With markers, draw a door on each piece. Hand out red paint and small branches for brushes. Let kids take turns painting the top and sides of one of the paper door frames. Have half the kids gather near the painted door frame and the other half near the unpainted door frame.

Have volunteers read Exodus 12:12-13 and 12:29-30. Invite children who enjoy role-playing to fall to the ground dramatically to show that some of the Egyptian people died. Invite the rest of the kids to act the way they think the people of that time acted when they discovered that the firstborn sons had died. Ask:

● **What would you have thought that night if you were an Egyptian? if you were an Israelite?**

● **Why did God let this happen?**

● **How do you think the king felt when he found out that the firstborn sons of the Egyptians had all died?**

● **What does this story teach us about God's protection?**

Say: **God provided protection for his people because they loved and obeyed him. God protected the people who wanted to worship him. God wanted the people to always remember that he provided protection. Let's see what God told them to do to help them remember.**

4 Always Remember

(You'll need crackers or matzos, cups of water, and a Bible.)

Have kids gather around a table where you've set out crackers or matzos and cups of water.

Say: **God told the people to get dressed as if they were going on a trip, then to eat the special Passover meal that night. God told the people to have a special meal every year to remember how he had protected them. We can remember that special time, too. Let's eat a snack now to remember the time God provided special protection for his people.**

While kids eat, read Exodus 12:8-17. Ask:

● **How did eating the meal this way help the people remember God's protection?**

● **Why is it good to have special times to remember what God has done?**

● **Why do you think God protects us?**

● **How has God protected you in the past?**

Say: **Let's thank God now for protecting the people of Israel and for loving and protecting us.**

5 Protection Prayer

(You'll need a Bible and markers.)

Gather children around the painted door frame. Say: **People in Bible times and people today ask God for protection. We need to be thankful when God protects us.**

Read Psalm 121:5-6 to the children: **"[God] himself is caring for you! He is your defender. He protects you day and night"** (The Living Bible). Have children write their names on the painted door frame to show that they need God's protection.

Say: **Let's say these verses from Psalms together. Then let's say this: "Right now we ask you to protect us from..." and you can add a word or two.**

Have kids repeat the verses from Psalms with you, phrase by phrase. Then add the sentence to the verse and have kids add a word or two.

Say: **We're thankful that God protected the people of Israel and that God protects us. I'm glad God loves and protects you.**

6 Recalling God's Protection

(You'll need Life Savers candy, twine, and scissors. Before class, cut twine into 2-foot lengths.)

Have kids sit in a circle.

Say: **God protects us in many ways, day after day, even when we don't think about it. Remembering good things God does for us is important. I'm going to pass around this roll of Life Savers. When the roll comes to you, take one Life Saver. Then tell about a time God protected you.**

If kids hesitate, start the discussion by sharing a time when God protected you. For example, "God protected me by helping the doctors discover why I was sick and what medicine I needed to get well" or "God protected me by helping me remember to wear my seat belt so that I wasn't hurt badly when another car hit mine."

Give everyone a chance to share, then ask:

● **Why is it important for us to think about God's protection?**

● **How does it make you feel when you think of ways God has protected you?**

Say: **God loved the people of Israel, so he protected them. God loves and protects us, too.**

Pass out pieces of twine. Have kids put their Life Savers on the twine and tie the twine around their necks to make necklaces.

Say: **Wear your necklace home as a reminder of God's protection. Let's give one final cheer of thanks for God's protection.**

Lead the kids in a quick, exuberant yell such as "Yea, God!"

LESSON 6
GOD'S GREAT POWER

Story: Crossing the Red Sea
Exodus 14:5-31

Good News: God uses his mighty power to help us.

The people of Israel had escaped from Egypt only to find themselves being pursued by the Egyptian king and his army. In their fright, the people wanted to go back to their Egyptian homes. Yet Moses stood strong against their opposition and continued to put his faith in God's mighty power. God showed this power by dividing the Red Sea so the people could cross to safety.

Just like the Israelites, we have a continuing need to be reassured that the Lord will fight for us. This lesson will help kids understand that God is willing to use his mighty power for us and deserves our thanks and rich praise.

A Look at the Lesson

1. Power Sources (10 minutes)—Kids will pantomime kinds of power and tell how power helps them.

2. Power Tag (15 minutes)—Students will play Power Tag and find out what a lack of power feels like.

3. God's Special Power (10 minutes)—Students will participate in the story told in Exodus 14 and see how God used his power to help the people of Israel.

4. Pow-Pow-Power! (10 minutes)—Kids will describe God's great power by creating TV or radio commercials, then read Psalm 21:13.

5. P Is for Power (10 minutes)—Children will describe the kinds of power God has given them.

6. Powerful Praise (5 minutes)—Kids will praise God for his power.

Preparation

Gather Bibles, a pencil, paper, and markers or crayons.

1 Power Sources

(You'll need slips of paper and a pencil.)

Before class, write these sources of power on separate slips of paper: electricity, gasoline engine, wind power, nuclear energy, muscle power. As children enter the classroom, welcome them and form pairs or groups of three or four. Give each group a slip.

Say: **With your group, think of a way to pantomime the kind of power written on your slip of paper. When it's your turn, act out the kind of power, and we'll guess what it is.**

Give kids about a minute to work out how they'll pantomime their sources of power. Then have groups take turns performing. After all groups have performed, ask:

● **Which kind of power is most important to you?**

● **How would our lives be different if we didn't have electricity? gasoline?**

● **What can these kinds of power be used for?**

Say: **Today we're going to talk about a special kind of power that** we haven't mentioned. **In fact, it's much more powerful than anything we've named so far. Any guesses about the kind of power I'm talking about?** Pause. **That's right—God's power!**

2 Power Tag

Say: **God's power is important because sometimes life makes us feel kind of powerless. Let's play a game to discover what that's like.**

Play a game of Power Tag. Designate one person as "It" and another as the "Power Maker." Players can only take baby steps, heel to toe. The Power Maker and It can take giant steps. Once kids are tagged by It, they have to freeze in place. If the Power Maker tags a frozen player, he or she can move again. Play for a few minutes, giving different kids the opportunity to be the Power Maker and It. Then gather everyone in a circle. Ask:

● **How did it feel to be chased by someone who could move a lot faster than you?**

● **When do you feel that way in real life?**

● **Who can tell about a time in real life when someone helped you the way the Power Maker helped you in this game?**

● **In the stories we've heard about the Israelites, how has God been like the Power Maker?**

Say: **You may remember that all the firstborn sons in Egypt died. But God protected his people. God told them to smear the blood of lambs on their doorposts—then they were safe. So finally, the king of Egypt let them go. But that wasn't the end of the story. Just as the Israelites were escaping, they turned around to find the Egyptian army following them! It wasn't a fair chase just as our game of Tag wasn't fair. The Egyptians drove fast chariots. The people of Israel were walking and had their children, animals, and all their belongings with them. They couldn't travel very fast. The people of Israel needed more power to escape, or they would be caught.**

Say: **Our Bible story in Exodus 14 tells us how the Israelites got that extra power. I want you to help me tell this exciting story.**

Practice each of these cues and responses with your class:

● **Whenever I say "king," boo.**

● **Whenever I say "Israelites," cheer.**

● **Whenever I say "Moses," stand and hold out your hand as if you're carrying a staff.**

● **Whenever I say "Lord," say, "Our God" and point to heaven.**

● **Whenever I say "chariots," move your hands in circles at your sides like wheels turning.**

● **Whenever I say "sea," put your hands together in front of you and make waves.**

As you read the following story taken from Exodus 14:5-18 and 21-31, emphasize the underlined words and pause to let kids respond. Keep the pace fast and exciting as you tell the story with great drama.

When the <u>king</u> of Egypt was told that the <u>Israelites</u> had left, he and his officers shook their heads. They said, "What have we done? We've let the <u>Israelites</u> leave. We've lost our slaves!" So the <u>king</u> jumped into his war <u>chariot</u> and took his army with him. He took 600 of his best <u>chariots</u>, together with all the other <u>chariots</u> of Egypt, and hundreds of soldiers. The <u>king</u> of Egypt was a stubborn man and still didn't want to let God's people go. The Egyptians—with all the <u>king's</u> horses, <u>chariot</u> drivers, and army—chased the <u>Israelites</u>. They caught up with them while they were camped by the Red <u>Sea</u>.

When the <u>Israelites</u> saw the <u>king</u> and his army coming after them, they were very frightened and cried to the <u>Lord</u> for help. They said to <u>Moses</u>, "What have you done to us? Why did you bring us out of Egypt to die in the desert? There were plenty of graves for us in Egypt. We told you in Egypt, 'Let us alone; we will stay and serve the Egyptians.' Now we will die in the desert."

But <u>Moses</u> answered, "Don't be afraid! Stand still and you will see the <u>Lord</u> save you today. You will never see these Egyptians again after today. You only need to remain calm; the <u>Lord</u> will fight for you."

Then the <u>Lord</u> said to <u>Moses</u>, "Why are you crying out to me? Command the <u>Israelites</u> to start moving. Raise your walking stick and hold it over the <u>sea</u> so that the <u>sea</u> will split and the people can cross it on dry land. When I defeat the <u>king</u>, his <u>chariot</u> drivers, and <u>chariots</u>, the Egyptians will know that I am the <u>Lord</u>."

Then <u>Moses</u> held his hand over the <u>sea</u>. All that night the <u>Lord</u>

drove back the <u>sea</u> with a strong east wind, so the water was split, and the <u>Israelites</u> went through on dry land, with a wall of water on their right and on their left.

Then all the <u>king's</u> horses and <u>chariots</u> followed them into the <u>sea</u>. Then the <u>Lord</u> told <u>Moses</u>, "Hold up your hand over the <u>sea</u> so that the water will come back over the Egyptians." So <u>Moses</u> raised his hand over the <u>sea</u>, and the walls of water came crashing down and covered all the <u>chariots</u> and soldiers. Not one of them survived.

So that day the <u>Lord</u> saved his people. The <u>Israelites</u> trusted the <u>Lord</u> and his servant <u>Moses</u>.

Have kids give themselves a round of applause for their participation in the story. Then ask:

● **How do you think you'd feel if you were walking and someone riding a horse started chasing you?**

● **What would you do to escape?**

● **How did God use his power to save the people of Israel?**

● **What did God want to prove to the Egyptians?**

Say: **The people of Israel wanted to serve God. But the king of Egypt wouldn't let them, so God helped his people escape from Egypt. They obeyed God by putting lambs' blood on their doorposts, then hurrying to escape. God used special power to protect the people who loved and obeyed him.**

Pow-Pow-Power!

(You'll need Bibles, paper, and markers or crayons.)

Say: **It's hard to imagine the greatness of God's power, but let's see if we can try.**

Set out paper and markers or crayons. Have kids work in groups of three or four to create radio or TV commercials that express the greatness and immensity of God's power. For example, "God is more powerful than a Saturn rocket. When you want to get somewhere, go with God!" "God's stronger than all the weight lifters on earth put together. God has a tower of power." Have groups work together for about three minutes, then perform their commercials. Ask:

● **How do you feel when you think of God's power?**

● **Why does God want to use his power to help us?**

● **When have you experienced God's power?**

If kids have difficulty thinking of something to share, tell of a time when you experienced God's power.

Say: **Your commercials have helped us get an idea of the greatness of God's power. Now let's look up a Bible verse that tells what we should do when we recognize God's power.**

Help kids find Psalm 21:13 in their Bibles, then read it aloud together.

Say: **God has mighty power, and God shares some of that power with us. Let's look at what God has given each of us.**

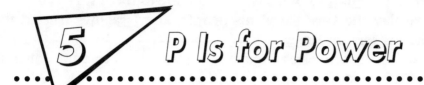

5 P Is for Power

Say: **Usually we think of power as a mighty force that moves things. But power can also be something that helps us do things well, or something that helps us be what God wants us to be. Let's explore how we experience that kind of power in our lives.**

Form pairs. Assign a letter from the word "power" to each group. Have pairs figure out a way to form their letters with their bodies. For example, a child could make a circle with his or her arms in front of his or her chest to make P. Or two kids could lie on the floor head to head and raise their legs and arms to form an E. While each pair is in its letter position, have other kids shout out ways the people forming the letters are powerful. For example, P might stand for great pal or patient. O might stand for outgoing or one of a kind. W might stand for wise or willing to do nice things. R might stand for ready to help or fast runner. Caution kids not to make negative comments about others.

After each pair has formed its letter, ask:

● **What other powers can you think of that group members might have that were not included in the letters we used?**

● **Why do you think God gives us these powers?**

● **How do you think God wants to use the powers and talents he gives us?**

Say: **It's good to recognize that God has given each of us special powers. It's also good to praise God for the power he uses to help and protect us, just as he protected the Israelites. Let's praise God together right now.**

Powerful Praise

Say: **Position yourself in a pose that shows as much power as possible. Hold that powerful pose as we pray.**

As kids hold their poses, lead them in a prayer similar to this one: **Dear God, we praise you for your mighty power. We thank you for the many ways you use your power to help us and protect us. Amen.**

LESSON 7
WHAT *IS* IT?

Story: The People Demand Food; God Sends Manna
Exodus 16:1-35
Good News: God provides for those who follow his instructions.

*T*he Israelites had been in slavery for many years. When God provided a way to freedom, they had to leave quickly, and they took very little food. As this lesson's story opens, the Israelites had been traveling in the desert for more than a month. The people were tired and had begun complaining. They actually started wishing they were back in Egypt, where they at least had plenty of food and water.

When the Israelites complained they didn't have enough to eat, God provided for them in a miraculous way. But along with God's provision came instructions, and the Israelites learned the hard way that they needed to listen and obey. This lesson will help kids understand that God provides for our needs, but we must obey God's instructions.

A Look at the Lesson

1. **Grumble Rumble** (7 minutes)—Students will list complaints and think about what complaining does.

2. **"God Provides" Pantomime** (12 minutes)—Kids will read the Bible story from Exodus 16 and act out how God provides for their needs.

3. **Manna Munchies** (12 minutes)—Students will eat pita bread or tortillas, listen to Exodus 16:31 and 35, and think about how the Israelites felt when they received manna.

4. **Manna Mix-Up** (12 minutes)—As they listen to Exodus 16:14-30, children will put together a puzzle to show how God's instructions fit together.

5. **Crumpled Complaints** (8 minutes)—Children will write down common complaints, crumple up the complaints, and listen to Philippians 4:6.

6. **Thank You** (9 minutes)—Kids will listen to 1 Peter 5:7, throw away their "complaints," and thank God for providing for their needs.

Preparation

Gather Bibles, newsprint, a marker, index cards, pencils, and a package of pita bread or tortillas. You'll also need a photocopy of the "Puzzle Pieces" handout (p. 54), paper, and a trash can.

1 Grumble Rumble

(You'll need newsprint and a marker.)

Form pairs. Say: **Decide which partner will be the listener and which will be the complainer. When I say "go," the complainers will name as many gripes as they can. These can be complaints about home, school, church—anything—but be sure not to gripe about people. I'll stop you in 60 seconds.**

Say: **Go.** After 60 seconds call time. Have partners switch roles for another 60 seconds of griping. Then gather the group together and invite kids to share the complaints and gripes they came up with. Write the complaints on newsprint. Then ask:

● **How did it feel to gripe to your partner?**

● How do you think others feel when you complain about them?

● Do you think we have more things to complain about than to be thankful for? Why or why not?

● What happens when you complain a lot?

● Does complaining help you or hurt you? Explain.

Say: **Everybody complains. But complaining rarely does any good. In fact, it can make us sad, and it can make us forget the good things God has given us. That's what happened to the people of Israel. Let's find out what happened when they griped to Moses.**

2 "God Provides" Pantomime

(You'll need Bibles, index cards, and pencils.)

Form two groups. Give group 1 two index cards and group 2 one index card. Give each group a pencil.

Say: **The Israelites had just seen God perform many miracles in Egypt. Now they were traveling through a desert, and they had a problem. Let's see what it was.**

Help kids turn to Exodus 16. Tell group 1 to read verses 1-5, and tell group 2 to read verses 6-12. Have group 1 write what it thinks the Israelites' main complaint was. Then have group 1 pass the card to group 2. Have group 2 write on the same card how God gave the people what they needed.

As kids read their verses, move from one group to another, helping them find their answers. For example, group 1 might find that the Israelites complained that

● they were very hungry,

● they had no food to eat, or

● they were starving to death.

Group 2 might find that God gave the people what they needed by

● making food fall like rain from the sky,

● sending enough food for everyone,

● giving the people food to pick up every day,

● providing bread each morning and meat each evening, or

● providing enough food for all the people every day.

Say to both groups: **Now, think of one way God provides for your needs. Write that on the other card. Plan how your group can act out what you wrote on your card in a pantomime.**

After the cards have been completed, call the groups back together and ask:

● **Why do you think the Israelites complained so much?**

● **How are the feelings of the Israelites like yours when you complain?**

● **How does God provide for our needs today?**

Have each group pantomime its modern-day example of how God provides for our needs. Have the other group guess what the kids are acting out. After each group has pantomimed, say: **God promises to take care of our needs. Let's see how God took care of the Israelites.**

(You'll need a Bible and pita bread or tortillas.)

Tear off a piece of the bread and pass it around for everyone to see, feel, and smell. While kids are passing it around, say: **God provided special food called manna. It fell from the sky, and the people gathered just enough to eat each day. Exodus 16:31 describes manna: "The people of Israel called the food manna. It was like small white seeds and tasted like wafers made with honey."**

Have someone read Exodus 16:35, then say: **When the people first saw manna, they didn't know what it was. They called it manna because manna means "What is it?" God provided manna for the people for 40 years!**

Tear off small pieces of bread and pass them around to the kids. As they eat their bread, ask:

● **What do you think the Israelites thought when Moses told them God would send food from heaven?**

● **How do you think the Israelites felt when food really did start coming down from heaven?**

Say: **God also gave the people instructions on how to collect and use the manna. Let's see what God said.**

4 Manna Mix-Up

(You'll need a Bible and a photocopy of the "Puzzle Pieces" handout. Cut out the puzzle pieces before class. To make the puzzle pieces easier for kids to handle, glue the handout to poster board or thin cardboard, then cut out the pieces.)

Sit with kids in a circle.

Say: **When God gave the people instructions on how to collect and** eat the manna, some obeyed and some didn't. The ones who didn't listen discovered that it's important to obey God. When the people trusted God and followed God's instructions, the people had everything they needed. Because God loves us, he tells us how to use what he gives us. Let's put a puzzle together to show how God fits everything together to provide for his people when they obey him.

Put the cut-apart puzzle pieces in the center of the circle with the printed sides facing up so the kids can read them.

Say: **I'll read some of the verses from Exodus that describe God's instructions to the Israelites and show their reactions.** (Name of person on your right) **has the first chance to find the correct puzzle piece to start the puzzle. Then the person on his** (or her) **right will find the second piece and fit it into the first puzzle piece.**

Read Exodus 16:14-30 aloud. Begin by reading Exodus 16:14-15 slowly. See if anyone identifies the Israelites' reaction and grabs a puzzle piece. If not, point out the correct piece to give kids get an idea of how the game works. Then read verse 16 and so on. Not every verse has a corresponding puzzle piece.

When the puzzle is completed, say: **God didn't put the Israelites' food in their cooking pots. The people had to collect the manna each day. God told them how to collect and use the manna. When the people followed God's instructions, they got what they needed.** Ask:

● **How do you think the people who didn't listen to God's instructions felt?**

● **How is fitting puzzle pieces together like fitting into God's plan?**

● **What can happen when you know what God wants you to do in a situation but you don't follow God's instructions very well?**

● **What can happen when you do follow God's directions?**

● **How does God provide for our needs through the instructions he gives us?**

Say: **God provides for our needs because he loves us. God's instructions help us get what we need. That's why God wants us to follow his instructions. God is pleased when we follow the instructions he gives us. Let's see how God wants us to handle our complaints.**

5 Crumpled Complaints

(You'll need a Bible, slips of paper, and pencils.)
Pass out paper and pencils.
Say: **Think of a time you complained, perhaps to your parents, a teacher, a friend, or even to God. Write that complaint on your piece of paper.**

After everyone has written something, say: **Now think about that complaint. Crumple up your paper and hold it tightly in your hand.**

Read Philippians 4:6, then ask:

● **How do you think God feels about our grumbling?**

● **Think of the complaint you have in your hand. What would happen if you held onto that complaint for the rest of the day?**

● **What's the best way to handle times when we feel like complaining?**

Say: **Complaining doesn't help us. It makes us feel discouraged. Instead, God tells us to give our worries and complaints to him. Let's find out one way we can give our complaints to God.**

6 Thank You

(You'll need a Bible and a trash can.)

Have kids stand in a circle, holding their crumpled papers with their complaints written on them. Place a trash can in the center of the circle.

Say: **Some people hang on to gripes for a long time, but it only hurts those people. To get rid of old grumbling and complaints, we can trust God to provide for our needs.**

Read 1 Peter 5:7, then ask:

● **What do you think God might want you to do with your worry or complaint?**

● **How will that help you in your situation?**

Say: **Thanking God for providing for our needs is one way we can learn to trust God to provide for our needs. To show that we're giving our complaints to God, let's thank God for providing what we need, then throw our complaints away.**

Lead the kids in a circle of prayer. With their heads bowed, have kids drop their complaints into the trash can and say sentence prayers asking God to help them bring their needs to God instead of complaining. Close with a prayer thanking God for giving us what we need.

Puzzle Pieces

54

LESSON 8
TRUSTING GOD FOR LITTLE THINGS

Story: God Provides Water From a Rock
Exodus 17:1-7
Good News: We can trust God for little things in our daily lives.

As the Israelites went further into the desert, they faced another survival crisis—no water! They complained to Moses, their leader. Even though God had kept them safe from the Egyptian army, guided them through the desert, and provided food in the form of manna, they grumbled because they had no water. God performed another miracle through Moses that teaches us the importance of trusting God with everyday problems.

Trusting God for our needs can be hard. In this lesson, kids will learn how to trust God with little things.

A Look at the Lesson

1. Waterless Lunch (12 minutes)—Kids will taste a meal made without water and think about why water is important.

2. Rocky Road (15 minutes)—Students will read Exodus 17:1-7 and act out a Bible story.

3. Trust Trek (10 minutes)—Kids will complete an obstacle course to learn about trust.

4. Cartoon Caper (10 minutes)—Children will draw cartoons of the lesson's Bible story and discuss why it's important to trust God.

5. Trust Tidbit (8 minutes)—Students will eat chocolate chips, read Proverbs 3:5, and tell how they will trust God for little things.

6. Trust-o-Gram (5 minutes)—Kids will each write one way they will trust God in the next week.

Preparation

You'll need Bibles, two packets of pre-sweetened fruit punch mix, one packet of dry soup mix, and one box of Jell-O. You'll also need prepared finger gelatin, a pitcher of water, glasses, plates, spoons, and napkins. Also, you'll need several squirt guns filled with water, a stick, tape, markers, newsprint, a bag of chocolate chips, envelopes, pencils, and photocopies of the "Trust-o-Gram" handout (p. 61).

1 Waterless Lunch

(You'll need two packets of pre-sweetened fruit punch mix, a packet of dry soup mix, a box of Jell-O, and prepared finger gelatin. To prepare the finger gelatin, add 1¼ cups boiling water to one large box of gelatin, mix thoroughly, and pour into an 8×8-inch pan. Chill for three hours and cut into cubes. Prepare fruit punch using one of the packets of drink mix and a pitcher of water. Hide the finger gelatin and fruit punch somewhere in the classroom before the children arrive. You'll also need glasses, plates, spoons, and napkins.)

Have kids sit around a table. Pass out glasses, plates, spoons, and napkins.

Say: **Today we're going to start with lunch. We'll have soup, Jell-O, and fruit punch.**

Put some dry fruit punch mix in each glass and some soup mix and dry Jell-O on each plate. Let kids taste their "waterless" meal. Ask:

● **What's wrong with this meal?**

● **How would your life be different if you didn't have much water?**

● **Water is a very simple thing. In what ways is water important to us?**

● **Imagine you were in a desert without any water. How would you feel?**

Say: **We can't live without water. Before we hear our Bible story, let's enjoy a snack made with water.**

Have kids empty the powdered mix from their glasses. Pour fruit punch into their glasses. Pass out the finger gelatin. Pray, thanking God for the food and for water. Enjoy the food, then have kids help clean up.

Say: **Today's story is about a time when the Israelites didn't have water to cook with or clean with or drink. Let's see what happened.**

(You'll need Bibles, a squirt gun filled with water, and a stick.)

Say: **God led the Israelites out of Egypt into the desert. The people grumbled and complained. First they complained about not having food, and God sent food from heaven. Then they complained about not having water.**

Help kids find Exodus 17:1-7. Have two volunteers alternate reading every other verse through all seven verses.

Then have volunteers play the parts of Moses, the rock, and the Israelites. Give the stick to Moses and the squirt gun to the rock. Have one good reader act as the narrator and read the passage. When verse 6 is read, have Moses gently tap the rock with the stick. Then have the rock squirt the squirt gun. Have kids change roles and act out the story again. Ask:

● **How do you think Moses felt when the people kept grumbling and complaining?**

● **How do you think God felt?**

● **Everyone complains sometimes. What do you complain about?**

● **How are the Israelites' complaints like your complaints?**

Say: **The Israelites had to trust that God would provide for them. Next, let's see how hard it is to trust someone.**

3 Trust Trek

(You'll need chairs and squirt guns filled with water.)

Arrange chairs in a complicated indoor obstacle course. Station several kids with squirt guns along the route. The object will be for guides to lead their partners through the obstacles without getting wet. Or, if possible, arrange an obstacle course outside using buckets of water and have guides lead their partners through the obstacles and past the squirt guns without getting wet.

Form pairs, then say: **When God led the Israelites to freedom, you'd think they would've trusted God easily. But they didn't. They grumbled and complained instead.**

Today we'll learn about trust by going on a "trust trek." One partner will guide, and the other will follow by walking backward without looking around. The guide will give the follower directions but cannot touch the follower. The follower has to rely on the directions the guide gives. Begin the trust trek.

If you have time, have kids switch roles and go through the course again. When everyone has completed the course, have kids sit in a circle. Ask:

● **How did you feel when you had to trust your partner to guide you?**

● **How might this be like the way the Israelites felt as they traveled in the desert with God guiding them?**

● **Why do you think it was hard for the Israelites to trust God?**

● **What are things that are hard for you to trust God with?**

● **What happens when you don't trust God?**

● **How could these situations turn out differently if you were to trust God?**

Say: **All of us struggle with trusting God. Let's draw cartoons that show how God protected his people. We can pretend that we'll use them to encourage the Israelites to trust God.**

4 Cartoon Caper

(You'll need Bibles, tape, markers, and three large pieces of newsprint.)

Before class, draw three large boxes on the newsprint. Tape the newsprint to the wall.

Say: **Let's make cartoons of Moses, the Israelites, and the water gushing from the rock. We'll have three teams, each drawing a picture from two verses that tell the story of God providing water.**

Form three teams. Designate one person on each team as the provider. The provider will give teammates markers as they need them. The teammates can't use markers unless the provider provides them.

Each team will work on one of the cartoon boxes. Team 1 will refer to Exodus 17:1-2 to portray the Israelites camping in the desert without water and grumbling to Moses. Team 2 will refer to verses 3 and 4 to portray the people coming to Moses with their complaints and Moses asking the Lord what to do. Team 3 will refer to verses 5 and 6 to portray Moses taking some of the older leaders and the walking stick to the rock, Moses striking the rock, and water gushing out.

After about six minutes of cartoon drawing, gather the group and let everyone look at the cartoon sequence. Then ask:

● **How did it feel to have a provider who gave you what you needed?**

● **How is this like Moses leading the Israelites?**

● **What do you think Moses was thinking when God told him to take the stick and hit a rock?**

● **When have you wondered if God was really right in wanting you to do something?**

● **The people asked, "Is the Lord with us or not?" Have you ever wondered if God was really with you? Explain.**

● **Why do you think it's important to trust God even when it seems hard or strange?**

Say: **The Israelites had a hard time trusting God to provide things like water and food, but God always provided them. God wants us to trust him for our needs, too—both the big and little things in our lives. Let's think about how we can trust God for the little things.**

5 Trust Tidbit

(You'll need a bag of chocolate chips.)

Have everyone sit in a circle. Put the bag of chocolate chips in the middle of the circle.

Say: **A tidbit is a tiny bit of something—something we eat, something we think about, or something we do. We can trust God with even the tidbits in our lives.**

Ask kids to turn to Proverbs 3:5 in their Bibles. Read the verse together.

Say: **God teaches us things all the time. God taught the Israelites to trust in him. They didn't have to worry about water; God provided them with everything they needed. God wanted them to trust in him for everything. Let's think about tidbits in our lives we can trust God with.**

Have kids each take a chocolate chip, tell about a tidbit they want to trust God with, then eat the chip. Some examples of "tidbit trusts" are trusting God for help on a test, being kind to a classmate who is hard to get along with, doing dishes without complaining, and remembering to do something nice for a parent.

Have several volunteers offer sentence prayers asking God to help them trust him more. Guide the kids in thanking God for his help and in asking God to help them trust him with little things each day.

Close by saying: **I thank you, God, for this group. Help each one of us to trust you every day. In Jesus' name, amen.**

6 Trust-o-Gram

(You'll need photocopies of the "Trust-o-Gram" handout, envelopes, and pencils.)

Give each person a photocopy of the "Trust-o-Gram" handout, an envelope, and a pencil.

Say: **We're each going to write a "Trust-o-Gram," which is like a telegram to God. Think of a problem, a challenge, or something you know God wants you to do or say this week. You might use one of the tidbit trusts you talked about earlier. Write it on the paper.**

After everyone has written something, have students fold their papers and place them in the envelopes. Have kids seal the envelopes and write their names and a date two weeks from today on them.

Say: **Take your envelope home, put it in a secret place, and open it on the date written on it to see if you trusted God with what you wrote on your Trust-o-Gram.**

Trust-O-Gram

Dear God,

A problem I have right now is

I need your help to

I would like to trust you more by

Thank you, God, for loving me. I love you and want to trust you more for the little things in my life.

Love,

LESSON 9
HELPING EACH OTHER

Story: Fighting the Amalekites
Exodus 17:8-15
Good News: We can help carry other people's burdens.

As the Israelites traveled in the desert, the Amalekites attacked them. Moses assembled soldiers and went to the top of a hill to watch the battle. He took the walking stick God had used to perform so many miracles. Whenever Moses raised his hands toward heaven, the Israelites began to win the battle. When Moses got tired and dropped his hands, the Amalekites started to triumph. Moses needed help so Aaron and Hur held up Moses' arms until the Israelites defeated their enemies.

Young children are taught easy ways to help others, such as making beds, cleaning the house, or helping a teacher erase a chalkboard. As children grow and mature, they discover more abstract methods of helping. They learn to help by praying for others, comforting them, or just listening.

In this lesson, students will recognize that God wants them to help carry others' burdens.

A Look at the Lesson

1. Making Swords (12 minutes)—Students will make swords and learn that helping one another makes things easier.

2. Sword Fight (10 minutes)—Students will have a mock battle while hearing a Bible story from Exodus 17:8-15.

3. Upraised Arms (10 minutes)—Kids will play a game with upraised arms, listen to Galatians 6:9-10, and discuss why helping is so important.

4. Too Heavy? Two Carry! (12 minutes)—Children will run a bucket relay, listen to Galatians 6:2, and discover that helping others makes burdens lighter.

5. Our Special Sword (12 minutes)—Kids will listen to Ephesians 6:17 and act out ways the Bible tells us to help others.

6. Raise Your Swords! (4 minutes)—Children will raise their swords and pray for people who need help.

Preparation

Gather Bibles, scissors, aluminum foil, tape, markers, 8½ × 11 pieces of cardboard, and photocopies of the "Sword Pattern" handout (p. 69). Also have available masking tape, a large stick, pencils, one large bucket filled with something heavy like dirt or gravel, a watch with a second hand, and one photocopy of the "Helping Friends" handout (p. 70).

1 Making Swords

(You'll need scissors, markers, aluminum foil, tape, 8½ × 11 pieces of cardboard, and photocopies of the "Sword Pattern" handout. Before class, place scissors and markers on a table in one corner of the room. To make an assembly line, put the aluminum foil in one corner, a table for molding foil in another corner, and tape in a third corner.)

Say: **Today we'll be learning about a battle God's people fought. In Bible times, people fought with swords, so we're going to make our own swords.**

Hand each child a photocopy of the "Sword Pattern" handout and one piece of cardboard. At the scissors table, have children cut out the sword pattern, trace the pattern on the cardboard piece, then cut out the traced figure. Have kids write their names on the handles and set their swords on the table.

Say: **Have you ever worked on a project at school when everyone was trying to use the same supplies? What a mess! Glue, scissors, and papers flying everywhere! Let's make our swords a different way.**

Form three teams. Have one team go to the corner where the aluminum foil is located, a second to the corner for molding, and the third to the tape corner. Let kids decide who will perform which functions at each corner. If you have twelve students or more, arrange two assembly lines.

Say: **We'll make our swords using an assembly line. The aluminum foil team will get a sword and measure and tear off enough foil to cover the blade—but not the handle—of the sword. Then the team will pass the sword to the molder team. This team will mold the foil onto the blade of the sword and carry it to the tape team. The tape team will tape the foil where it meets the handle and set the finished sword back on the first table. Organize your teams and begin the assembly line.**

When the assembly line has completed all the swords, gather kids in a circle. Ask:

● **Do you think helping one another made it easier to complete the swords? Why or why not?**

● **What's something you do every day that's easier to finish with help?**

● **Think of a time when someone helped you with something. What would've happened if you had done it alone?**

Say: **It was fun to help each other complete this project on our assembly line. Today we're going to find out how God's people won a battle because two people helped Moses.**

 **Sword Fight**

(You'll need masking tape, a large stick, and the handmade swords.)

Place a strip of masking tape down the center of the room. Choose three children to play the parts of Moses, Aaron, and Hur. Form two groups with the rest of the children. Call one group the Amalekites and the other group the Israelites. Gather the Amalekites on one side of the tape and the Israelites on the other side. Distribute the swords to everyone but Moses, Aaron, and Hur. Give the stick to Moses and place a large chair nearby.

Say: **As I read the Bible story, pretend to fight with your swords in slow motion. Watch Moses, Aaron, and Hur. When Moses raises his arms, the Israelites are to step over the taped line and the Amalekites are to back up. When Moses' hands are down, the Amalekites are to step over the line as the Israelites back up.**

Read the following story from Exodus 17:8-15. Pause at appropriate places to allow the children to act it out.

Say: **One day the Amalekites came to fight the Israelites.** Pause. **Moses, Aaron, and Hur went to the top of a nearby hill to watch the battle.** Pause. **At the beginning of the fight, Moses took his walking stick and raised his hands to heaven.** Pause. **As he did so, the Israelites started to win.** Pause. **But soon Moses' arms grew tired, and he put his hands down to rest.** Pause. **Then the Israelites began to lose the battle.** Pause. **Moses forced his hands up again, but he didn't have the strength to keep them up, so down they fell again.** Pause.

Then Aaron and Hur had an idea. They rolled a large stone over to Moses and had him sit down. Have Moses sit in the chair. **Aaron stood on one side of Moses, and Hur stood on the other side. They grabbed his hands and lifted them high in the air.** Pause. **The Israelites started winning again.** Pause. **Aaron and Hur helped Moses keep his arms up until the sun went down and the Amalekites were completely defeated! Afterward, Moses built an altar and thanked God for helping them win.**

Gather the kids in a circle. Then ask:

● **How do you think Moses felt when he realized his army was losing because he couldn't keep his hands in the air?**

● **How do you think Moses felt when Aaron and Hur helped him?**

● **What would've happened if Aaron and Hur had not helped Moses?**

● **How is what Aaron and Hur did like what we can do when we see someone who has a problem?**

Say: **Just as Aaron and Hur helped Moses, we can lift others' spirits and encourage them. Let's see what can happen when we don't help others.**

3 Upraised Arms

(You'll need a Bible.)

Form groups of three. Designate half the groups as helpers and the other half as cheerleaders.

Say: **Select one person in your group to be the "arm raiser." In the helper groups, team members will help the arm raiser keep his or her arms up and will also cheer for the arm raiser. In the cheerleader groups, team members will cheer for the arm raiser, but they can't help hold his or her arms up.**

Say: **Go.** Encourage team members to cheer the arm raisers by saying, "Keep it up!" "You can do it!" or "You're doing great!" Keep cheering until most of the cheerleaders' arm raisers have dropped their arms. Then have everyone else lower their arms. Ask:

● **If you were an arm raiser in a cheerleader group, how did it feel when your team members cheered for you but didn't help?**

● **If you were an arm raiser in a helper group, how did it feel to have your team members hold up your arms?**

● **Why does it feel so good to be helped and to help others?**

Have a volunteer read Galatians 6:9-10. Ask:

● **If you were in a helper group, did you get tired of helping? If so, why?**

● **What should we do when we get tired of helping?**

Say: **We don't always feel like helping. Sometimes we get tired of doing good. Aaron and Hur might have gotten tired of holding Moses' arms up for a long time. But they didn't give up until the Israelites had won the battle. Let's see what can happen when people help each other.**

4 Too Heavy? Two Carry!

(You'll need a Bible, a watch with a second hand, and one large bucket filled with something heavy like dirt or gravel.)

Form two groups. Send the groups to opposite sides of the room. Have groups line up for a relay race. Set the bucket in front of one group.

Say: **We're going to do two different bucket relays. I'll time them both to see which takes the least amount of time. For the first relay, the first person in line must carry the bucket to the first person in line on the other side of the room. Then that person must carry it back. Keep going until everyone has carried the bucket. I'll keep track of how long it takes. Ready, Go!**

Time the relay. When it's over, have all the kids gather on one side of the room for the second relay. Have a volunteer read Galatians 6:2. Form pairs and have kids line up.

Say: **We're going to have one more relay. Only this time, instead of each person carrying the bucket alone, partners will help each other carry the bucket. To make the total distance traveled by the entire group the same as in the first relay, each pair will go to the other side, touch the wall, come back, and give the bucket to the next pair in line. Ready? Go!**

Time the relay. Compare the times. Gather the kids in the center of the room. Tell them how much faster the second relay was than the first. If the second relay was slower, emphasize how much easier and more fun it was to carry the bucket with a partner. Ask:

● **How difficult was it when you carried the bucket alone?**

● **How is this like having a problem in your life but not having anyone to help you with it?**

● **How did you feel the second time when you had help carrying the bucket?**

● **How is this like when we help those who are troubled or who have problems?**

Say: **When we see people struggling through situations, God wants us to help them. Sometimes the loads they're carrying are too heavy to carry alone. Helping people with their troubles makes their troubles seem lighter, just as the bucket seemed lighter when two people carried it. The Bible shows us ways to help one another. Let's read about some of them.**

5 Our Special Sword

(You'll need Bibles, pencils, scissors, and a photocopy of the "Helping Friends" handout cut apart on the dotted lines.)

Say: **We have a special sword that can help us know how God wants us to help others.**

Read Ephesians 6:17.

Say: **The Bible is the sword of the Spirit. It tells us different ways we can help people. Let's find out what some of them are.**

Form groups of three. Have each group choose one member as a recorder. The other two members will be actors. Give each group a Bible, a pencil, and a section of the "Helping Friends" handout.

Say: **Read the situation and look up the Bible passage. Using the verse as a guide, the actors will act out one way to help the person in this situation. The recorder will write a title for the scene the actors will act out. For instance, if the verse talks about praying for someone, act out what you could say in your prayer. The recorder might call it "A Helping Prayer."**

After the groups have had time to prepare, read the situations one at a time. Have the recorders give their titles and the actors act out their helping scenes.

Say: **As we help others, we become God's helpers here on earth. Let's practice one way of helping others: praying for them.**

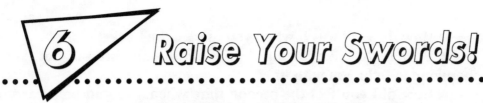

6 Raise Your Swords!

(You'll need the handmade swords.)

Gather in a circle. Take prayer requests from kids about their own needs or those of people they know.

Say: **To help us remember that we can use the sword of the Spirit to help others, let's raise our swords as we pray.**

Have the children point their swords with tips toward heaven and pray for the requests mentioned.

Sword Pattern

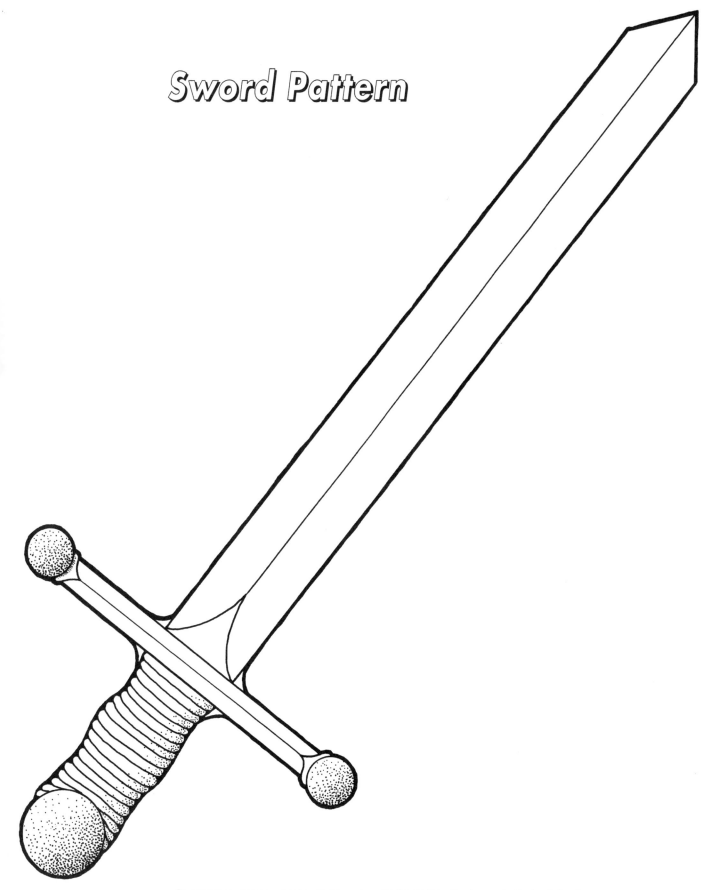

HELPING FRIENDS

You're at an arcade and notice Johnny walking around from game to game, just watching and not playing. You know his parents don't have much money, and your mom just gave you $5 to spend.

How could you help in this situation?

Look up Matthew 6:3-4.

Write your title here: _____

Act out one way to help Johnny in this situation.

A friend's parents have just gone through a divorce. Your friend lives with his mom, but he really misses his dad.

How could you help in this situation?

Look up Isaiah 66:13.

Write your title here: _____

Act out one way to help your friend in this situation.

A friend tried out for the soccer team, but he found out he didn't make the team. He's been depressed ever since.

How could you help in this situation?

Look up Ephesians 4:29.

Write your title here: _____

Act out one way to help your friend in this situation.

A friend sees your Bible, looks puzzled, and asks why you read it.

How could you help in this situation?

Look up Acts 8:35.

Write your title here: _____

Act out one way to help your friend in this situation.

There's a girl in your classroom at school who's always alone. No one will have anything to do with her because she's too shy to be friendly.

How could you help in this situation?

Look up Matthew 7:12.

Write your title here: _____

Act out one way to help the girl in this situation.

LESSON 10
MORE THAN A RULE BOOK

Story: The Ten Commandments
Exodus 20:1-21

Good News: Out of love, God gives us rules to follow.

Moses led the people out of their camp in the desert to the base of Mount Sinai. The mountain was covered with smoke and shook violently. God called to Moses from the mountain, and Moses climbed the slopes to meet with God. None of the other Israelites except Aaron were allowed to follow Moses because the mountain was holy.

On Mount Sinai, God gave Moses the Ten Commandments to deliver to the people of Israel. In these commandments, God reveals his character and gives us a way to express love for God and for one another.

At first, middle-elementary children may think some of God's commandments are restricting and unnecessary. This lesson will help kids discover the importance of rules and how God expresses love for us through the Ten Commandments.

A Look at the Lesson

1. Right Rules (10 minutes)—Kids will write down rules and talk about why rules are important.

2. Balloon Blow (15 minutes)—Students will play a balloon game, read the Ten Commandments, listen to John 14:15, and tell how they will obey God.

3. Maze o' Life (10 minutes)—Kids will go through a maze blindfolded to learn about following rules.

4. Measuring Up (10 minutes)—Children will follow rules to make peanut butter balls, listen to Luke 11:28, and discuss how God's rules are the standard to measure their actions by.

5. Current Events (10 minutes)—Students will clip articles from newspapers, listen to 1 John 1:9, and talk about what happens when we don't follow God's rules.

6. Love Notes (5 minutes)—Kids will write love notes to God and make a commitment to follow one of God's commandments.

Preparation

Gather a Bible, a marker, pencils, masking tape, construction paper, a blindfold, a balloon, a cassette player, and a cassette tape of lively music. You'll also need newsprint or a chalkboard and chalk, measuring cups, wax paper, mixing spoons, and mixing bowls. Bring powdered sugar, powdered milk, peanut butter, moist towels, a current newspaper, scissors, and tape.

1 Right Rules

(You'll need a marker, pencils, tape, and construction paper.)

Before class, write one heading on four pieces of construction paper: "At Home," "At School," "At Church," "At Play." Tape one sign near each corner of the room.

As kids enter the classroom, give them each a piece of construction paper and a pencil. Form groups of four. Have kids in each group number off from one to four. Send the ones to one corner, the twos to another corner, and so on.

Say: **When the lights flash, you'll have three minutes to write down a list of rules you follow at the place written on the sign.**

Flash the lights. After three minutes, flash the lights again and have kids return to their original groups.

Say: **Share the rules you wrote with your group members.**

Allow a few minutes for each person to share. Then form one big group and ask volunteers to share what they wrote. Ask:

● **Why do you think we have rules in all these places?**

● **What might happen if we didn't have rules?**

● **Is it easy or hard for you to follow rules? Why?**

Say: **God has rules for us to follow. We follow God's rules because God is good and his rules are good for us. Let's find out 10 important rules God wants us to obey. In the Bible, these 10 rules are called commandments.**

Balloon Blow

(You'll need a Bible, one balloon, masking tape, a cassette player, and a cassette tape of upbeat music.)

Before class, blow up the balloon. Have kids form one big circle. Open a Bible to Exodus 20 and place the Bible in the center of the circle.

Say: **When you hear the music, begin passing the balloon. You may hold it by the tied end only. Pass it around the circle. Whoever has the balloon when the music stops must read one of the commandments God gives us in Exodus 20:3-17.**

Start the music. After a few seconds, stop the music and have the child with the balloon go to the Bible and find a commandment in Exodus 20:3-17, read it, and return to the circle. Start the music again and have the kids pass the balloon again. When all of the Ten Commandments have been read, ask:

● **Which commandment is the most important? Why?**

● **Why do you think we should try to keep God's commandments?**

Read John 14:15. Say: **God gave us the Ten Commandments because he loves us. God gave us these rules because he knows that doing wrong things weighs us down. We show our love to God by obeying his commandments. When we obey God, we might feel as light as this balloon. Let's play a game of Balloon Blow to help us remember that God's rules keep us from being weighted down by wrong actions.**

Put a masking tape line on the floor. Form two teams. Have each team stand in a line parallel to the tape.

Choose a volunteer to begin the game. Toss the balloon in the air over the tape line. As it comes down, the first person will complete the sentence "I will obey God by _____" and will blow the balloon to someone across the tape. If the balloon touches the floor, pick it up and resume the game from that spot. Play the game until everyone has had a chance to complete the sentence.

Say: **Rules are directions that help us no matter where we are. Let's find out how important it is to listen to and follow rules and directions.**

3 Maze o' Life

(You'll need a blindfold.)

Use furniture to create a maze in the classroom that will take kids under a table, around a chair, and along a wall. Have kids pair up and number off from one to two. Give the first pair the blindfold.

Say: **All ones are guides, and all twos are followers. Each follower will have one turn to get through the maze. Kids not going through the maze will be the crowd. The follower will be blindfolded. The guide _and_ the crowd will tell the follower how to get through the maze from the sidelines. I will point to the guide or the crowd to silently show which one will give the _right_ directions. The follower won't know if the guide or the crowd is giving the right directions. Guides can use whatever words he or she chooses, but the crowd can say only "hot" to indicate that the follower is going in the right direction or "cold" to indicate that the follower is going the wrong way. Followers will decide whose directions to follow.**

After the first follower is blindfolded, silently indicate whether the guide or the crowd will tell the follower the right directions. After all the followers have gone through the maze, ask:

● **If you were a follower, how did you decide whose guidance to listen to?**

● **How important is it to follow directions carefully? Explain.**

● **What happens when you follow the wrong rules?**

Say: **Sometimes it's hard to know how to follow rules. Some people would give us rules that aren't good to follow. Let's see how to tell if rules measure up.**

4 Measuring Up

(You'll need a Bible, newsprint and a marker or chalkboard and chalk, measuring cups, wax paper, mixing spoons, mixing bowls, powdered sugar, powdered milk, peanut butter, and moist towels.)

> **PEANUT BUTTER BALLS**
>
> ¼ cup powdered sugar
> ¼ cup powdered milk
> ½ cup peanut butter
> Recipe serves four.

Write the recipe ingredients on newsprint or a chalkboard. Form groups of four. Give each group a measuring cup, a mixing spoon, a mixing bowl, and a sheet of wax paper. Place all the ingredients on a table where kids can measure out what they need.

Say: **Today we're going to make a special treat. First, measure the ingredients as listed on the chalkboard and put them in your bowl. If you have a ¼-cup measuring cup, fill your ¼ cup two times to make ½ cup. If you have a ½-cup measuring cup, fill it halfway to measure ¼ cup. When you've finished measuring your ingredients, return to your table and wait for further directions.**

After everyone has measured the ingredients, give the following directions, allowing enough time for groups to complete each step: **Step 1: Mix the sugar, powdered milk, and peanut butter together. Step 2: Form the mixture into four balls. Step 3: Place the peanut butter balls on a sheet of wax paper.**

Have the children wipe their hands with moist towels then enjoy the snack while you discuss these questions:

● **Why do you think it was important to use measuring cups for this recipe?**

● **How are measuring cups like God's rules?**

● **Why is it important for us to have God's standards to measure ourselves by?**

Say: **God helps us measure our thoughts and actions by the standard he gives us in his Word.**

Have a volunteer read Luke 11:28.

Say: **God gave us commandments to help us. When we listen to and follow God's guidance, we find peace and happiness. But sometimes it's difficult to follow God's rules.** Ask:

● **What obstacles stand in the way of obeying God's rules?**

● **How can we overcome the obstacles that keep us from following**

God's rules?

Say: **Let's look at ways people disobey God's rules.**

5 Current Events

(You'll need a Bible, a current newspaper, pencils, and scissors.)

Form trios. Give each trio a section of the newspaper, a pencil, and scissors. Have each group choose one person to be the finder, one to be the clipper, and one to be the recorder.

Say: **Find situations in the newspaper in which people disobeyed one of God's commandments.**

Show the kids an example, such as a person who lied in court or someone who stole money.

Then say: **Cut out as many articles as you can find. The finder will find the articles, and the clipper will cut them out. The recorder will write the commandment on each article. You have three minutes. Go!**

When time is up, call the class together and have the recorders share their findings. Ask:

● **Does the world measure up to God's standards? Why or why not?**

● **What did you learn from the articles about the importance of obeying God's commandments?**

Say: **These newspaper articles help us see that not everyone follows God's commandments. In fact, none of us follows the rules perfectly all the time. But God has provided a way to help us when we disobey his rules.**

Read 1 John 1:9. Ask:

● **How do you think God feels when we blow it and don't measure up to the standards he's given us?**

● **What does this verse say we can do when we disobey God's rules?**

Say: **God shows love to us by giving us rules that help us live. We show love to God by obeying his commandments. But even when we mess up, God gives us a way to make it right. When we blow it, we can ask for God's forgiveness, and he'll give it to us because he loves us and he promised that he would forgive us. This week let's show our love to God by promising to follow one commandment.**

6 Love Notes

(You'll need red construction paper, scissors, tape, and pencils.)

Before class, cut enough large hearts from red construction paper for each student to have one. Pass out pencils and hearts.

Say: **Let's make love notes to God. On your heart, write one of the Ten Commandments that's hard for you to obey. Then write how you'll obey it this week. It could be something you'll do at home, at school, at church, or while you're with friends. For instance, you might write, "Honor your father and mother." Then you might write, "I'll answer my mother with a kind voice when she asks me to do a chore." When you're finished, ask God to help you obey this commandment. Fold your heart in half and tape it closed. Take your love note home and put it beside your bed to remind you to obey the commandment.**

When kids finish their love notes, close in prayer. Ask God to help your students obey God's commandments and thank God for showing love to us by giving us commandments to follow.

LESSON 11

DOING WHAT'S RIGHT

Story: God Gives Us Rules About Treating Others Fairly
Exodus 23:1-9

Good News: Treating others fairly is the right thing to do.

Much of the Bible speaks to the issue of dealing with one another fairly. Jesus said that the second most important commandment is to love our neighbors as we love ourselves. Paul says that we'll be judged by the same rules with which we judge others. The emphasis is on treating people well. The Bible passage chosen for this lesson, Exodus 23:1-9, shows how important it is to treat others fairly.

This lesson will help middle-elementary kids discover that treating others fairly is an important choice they can make.

A Look at the Lesson

1. Eggs-ercise (10 minutes)—Kids will play a game and discover that being treated fairly makes the game more fun.

2. Fair Play (10 minutes)—Students will read about unfair situations and decide how to handle them.

3. Get the Scoop (8 minutes)—Kids will feed partners a snack while blindfolded, listen to Psalm 119:2, and learn that God takes the guesswork out of following his rules.

4. Here Comes the Judge (15 minutes)—Students will have a court judge various situations, read Exodus 23:1-9, and think about God's fair rules.

5. Simple Choices (12 minutes)—Students will each choose a bag with a prize in it, read 1 John 3:18, and talk about how they can choose to treat others fairly.

6. Amen! (5 minutes)—Children will ask God to help them treat others fairly.

Preparation

You'll need Bibles, a watch with a second hand, a dropcloth, raw eggs, two hard-boiled eggs, paper bags, scissors, pencils, and photocopies of the "Fair Play" handout (p. 85). Also gather mini–fish crackers, paper cups, spoons, blindfolds, paper towels, and cups of water. You'll also need a stapler, slips of paper, a variety of small items for prizes, and a photocopy of the "Here Comes the Judge" handout (p. 86).

1 Eggs-ercise

(You'll need a watch with a second hand, a dropcloth, one raw egg for every two kids, and two hard-boiled eggs.)

This activity works best outdoors. If you do it indoors, cover the floor with a dropcloth.

Have kids form pairs. Then form two lines with partners facing each other about six feet apart. Give each pair an egg, making sure two pairs get the hard-boiled eggs. Don't tell the kids that there's a difference in the eggs.

Say: **The object of this game is to get your egg to your partner without breaking it. Those of you on this side** (point to one side) **can use your hands to toss the egg, but the rest of you must get the egg to** your partner without using your hands. You can use your feet or arms or roll the egg on the ground (or floor) with your nose. If you get the egg to your partner, take a large step backward. But if the egg drops and breaks, you and your partner are sidelined until the game ends. The people on the sidelines are to cheer for the other pairs. The two pairs that are the farthest apart with their eggs still intact when I call time are the winners. Ready? Go!

After a minute and a half, reverse the roles without warning so that those who could use their hands at the game's outset must find another way to deliver the eggs. After another minute and a half, call time.

Make a big production of congratulating the winners. Then reveal that two pairs had hard-boiled eggs. Gather kids into one group and ask:

● **What was unfair about this game?**

● **How did you feel when you found out that two pairs had hard-boiled eggs?**

● **How did you like having the rules changed without warning in the middle of the game?**

● **Why is it important for everyone to play by the same rules?**

● **How is this game like situations in real life?**

Say: **We all know how it feels to be treated unfairly, and none of us likes it. Even though we know how bad it feels, sometimes we treat others unfairly. Treating others fairly takes work, so we're going to practice treating each other with fairness.**

(You'll need scissors, pencils, a paper bag, and photocopies of the "Fair Play" handout.)

Cut apart the sections of the handout and put them in a paper bag. It's OK to use the same situation in more than one group.

Form groups of four and give each group a pencil. Have each group choose one member as the picker, one as the reader, another as the recorder, and the fourth as the sharer. Have the picker pick a slip from the paper bag. The reader will read the slip, and the recorder will write notes on the back of the slip. Allow two minutes for kids to decide what they would do in the situation they picked. When two minutes are up, gather the groups together. Have the reader in each group read the group's situation and the sharer share the group's decision. After each group finishes, have kids from other groups tell how they might have handled the situation. Ask:

● **Which person in these situations could you identify with most? Why?**

● **How do you feel when you're treated unfairly?**

● **What have you done when you've seen someone else treated unfairly?**

● **Why is it important to treat others fairly?**

● **Why do you think it's important to God that we treat others fairly?**

Say: **Sometimes we know exactly what to do to treat others fairly. Other times, we don't know how to do things right. Let's see what happens when we aren't sure we're doing things right.**

3 Get the Scoop

(You'll need a Bible, mini–fish crackers, a paper cup for each pair, one spoon and one blindfold for each student, paper towels, and cups of drinking water.)

Form pairs. Pass out spoons and blindfolds to everyone and give each pair a cup of mini–fish crackers.

Say: **This is a contest to see which pair can eat the fish crackers the fastest. One person in each pair will begin by feeding his or her partner fish crackers with a spoon while both of you are blindfolded. When you hear me say "reverse," switch roles. Each time I say "reverse," switch roles again.**

As soon as all the kids have their blindfolds on, begin. When one pair has eaten all its crackers, stop the game. Let the rest of the kids finish their fish crackers without blindfolds, then have everyone help clean up the mess. Offer cups of water to those who are thirsty. Gather kids in a circle and ask:

● **What was it like trying to feed your partner blindfolded?**

● **How is this like trying to follow directions without knowing what to do?**

● **How can we learn more about what God says?**

Read Psalm 119:2.

● **Why do you think we are happier when we follow God's rule by treating others fairly?**

Say: **You had to do a lot of guessing in this game. Sometimes treating others fairly seems like guesswork. But God takes the guesswork out of knowing how to treat others fairly by giving us specific guidelines to follow. We're going to learn more about these right now.**

Here Comes the Judge

(You'll need Bibles, a photocopy of the "Here Comes the Judge" hand-out, pencils, and scissors. Cut apart the sections of the handout and put them in a paper bag.)

Ask for a volunteer to be the judge. Have kids form pairs and give each pair a pencil. The judge's partner will be part of the jury until a new judge is appointed.

Say: **Each pair will be given a situation to present to the judge. Kids who aren't presenting a situation will be the jury. The jury will decide whether or not a crime has been committed. The judge will then decide the appropriate punishment or reward.**

Have each pair draw one slip from the bag. Say: **You and your partner have three minutes to come up with an idea that completes the sentence about your situation. You will present your situation to the judge. Then the jury will vote by saying "yea" if they think a crime has been committed and "nay" if they think no crime has been committed. The judge will announce the appropriate punishment or reward.**

Encourage the judge to declare extravagant and humorous punishments and rewards; for example, having to do dishes in a clown suit every night for a year for telling a lie, or being honored in a parade on Main Street for showing kindness to someone who acted mean.

After three minutes, ask for volunteers to present their situation to the judge. After each situation has been presented and voted on, appoint a new judge.

After all pairs have presented, ask:

● **What was it like to go in front of the judge to be rewarded or punished?**

● **What would you have done if the judge or jury had treated you unfairly?**

● **How was this activity like not knowing if people will treat you fairly in real life?**

Say: **God's rules for treating people are written in the Bible. We can use God's rules as a guideline on how to treat our friends, parents, teachers, or anyone. Let's look at some of God's rules.**

Have volunteers read Exodus 23:1-9 aloud. In their pairs, have kids write on the back of their slips the Bible verses from Exodus 23:1-9 that match their situations. Ask:

● **How does it help you to know what God expects of you?**

● **Now that you've read these verses, how will you treat others more fairly?**

Say: **God is a just and righteous judge. God loves us so much that he wants to make sure we know how to treat others. Treating others fair-**

ly makes our lives better and helps those around us, too. God wants us to treat others fairly, but we choose whether or not to obey God.

5 Simple Choices

(You'll need a stapler; lunch bags; slips of paper numbered from one through six; and a variety of small items such as pencils, stickers, and fun-shaped erasers.)

Place one item in each bag, then staple the bags closed. Using different-colored or decorated bags will make this activity more exciting. You may heighten the suspense by adding two odd prizes such as a gum wrapper without any gum inside or an old sock. Tell kids that there are two bags with odd prizes in them.

Have kids sit in a circle on the floor. Place the bags in the center of the circle. Pick a number between one and 100. Have kids each pick a number and tell you what they chose. Whoever comes closest to the number you picked will go first. Put the slips of paper with the numbered sides down in the center of the circle.

Say: **Draw a slip of paper. If it has an even number on it, you get to pick a bag from the middle of our circle or take an already-picked bag from someone else. Put the bag in front of you, but don't open it. If the slip of paper has an uneven number on it, you must pass and the person on your right has the next turn.**

Have kids cheer each other on by saying things like "Take the red bag" or "What a fast chooser!" or "I know you got a good prize in your bag." End the game when everyone has a bag. Let kids open their bags. Ask:

● **Why did you pick the bag you picked?**

● **How did you feel when you saw your prize?**

Say: **Choosing a bag is a simple choice. We make lots of choices every day. Deciding to treat others fairly is also a choice.** Ask:

● **What kind of consequences might happen if you make the wrong choice and treat others badly?**

● **What good things can happen when you treat others fairly?**

Say: **In this game, we chose the bag we wanted. We also choose how we treat others. The choices we make determine whether we obey or disobey God's Word. Let's read a verse that tells us how to make good choices.**

If you had odd prizes in two bags, say: **To demonstrate that we want to treat others fairly, I'll give a good prize to the students who got the odd ones.** Give good prizes to the two children who got the odd ones.

Read 1 John 3:18. Ask:

● **How can you use this verse to treat others fairly?**

● **What do you think true caring means?**

● **Think about a time when you practiced true caring. How did it make you feel?**

● **How did it make the other person feel?**

Say: **True caring means treating others fairly. God will help us practice true caring.**

6 Amen!

Say: **Let's ask God to help us treat others fairly every day this week. For example, you might pray, "God, help me treat others fairly by not telling lies, by showing kindness to new people at school, and by not saying bad things about others."**

Have volunteers pray. When everyone who wants to has prayed, close by thanking God for rules that help us know how to treat each other fairly.

Say: **Take your prize home and put it where it'll remind you to treat others fairly.**

FAIR PLAY

Photocopy this handout and cut apart the sections.

Sally, Jennifer, and Melissa are three friends who enjoy playing together at Melissa's house. One day, while the kids are playing, Melissa gets to be first three times in a row. Finally, it's Jennifer's turn, but Melissa wants to play a different game. When Jennifer objects, Melissa says, "It's my house, so I get to do what I want." What would you do if you were Sally?

Robbie, Will, and Beau are best buddies. One day, Robbie is riding his bike past Will's house and sees Beau's bike parked in the driveway. Robbie goes to the door and rings the bell. Will and Beau come to the door. Robbie asks what they are doing, and Will says they are playing basketball in the back yard. Robbie asks if he can play, too. Will says, "No, we don't want to play with you anymore. Bye!" and shuts the door. What would you do if you were Beau?

You're trying out for a part in the school play. You've always wanted to star in a play and are excited about being involved. Two other kids also try out for the main character. One of them is a very good actor. The teacher gives you a copy of the script ahead of time. Now you'll have more time to practice than the others and will probably do a better job at the tryouts. What will you do?

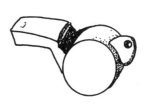

HERE COMES THE JUDGE

Photocopy this handout and cut apart the sections.

You've been telling lies to your parents about...

At school, you've been ganging up on someone by...
because everyone else is doing it.

You've shown kindness to someone at school by...
even when he's been really mean to you.

You've been teasing a kid at school by...
because his family doesn't have money to buy new clothes for him.

You helped a bully on your street by...

You took money from your friend who wanted you to lie about...

A student from China was visiting your class
and you made fun of her by...

LESSON 12
SHINE ON!

Story: The Golden Calf
Exodus 32:1-24, 30-32
Good News: As we overcome temptation, our lights will shine for God.

When Moses didn't return quickly from Mount Sinai, the Israelites became impatient and asked Aaron to make a god for them to worship. Aaron gave in to their pressure and formed a golden calf made from their jewelry. Despite God's faithfulness to them, the Israelites gave in to temptation as soon as it confronted them.

Since sin entered the world, people have struggled with temptation. Yet God, through Jesus, gives us strength to fight temptation. In this lesson, children will learn that they should stand strong against temptation. When they do, others will see God's light in their lives.

A Look at the Lesson

1. How Great Thou Art (10 minutes)—Students will see how hard it is to keep their minds on God.

2. Picture This (15 minutes)—Kids will read Exodus 32:1-24 and 30-32, create hieroglyphics, and find out what happened when the Israelites took their minds off God.

3. God Cures Temptation's Lures (10 minutes)—Kids will pass around a fishing lure, listen to 1 Corinthians 10:13, and tell how God will help them deal with temptations.

4. Let Your Light Shine (10 minutes)—Students will light candles and talk about being lights for God.

5. Keep That Flame Burning (10 minutes)—Students will put construction paper flames on a city map and decide how they'll be lights for God.

6. Candy-Corn Prayer (5 minutes)—Kids will hold up a candy "flame" and ask God to help them shine their lights this week.

Preparation

Gather Bibles, newsprint, 3×5 cards, markers, tape, a fishing lure, birthday candles, aluminum foil, and matches. Also bring a city map, scissors, red or yellow construction paper, candy corn or yellow gumdrops, and photocopies of the "Picture This" handout (p. 93).

1 How Great Thou Art

Lead the kids outside and invite them to concentrate on God's wonderful creation. Have them point out what they see. If the weather isn't suitable to take the children outside, bring objects from nature to the classroom, such as branches, feathers, or leaves—items that kids can see, touch, and smell.

Say: **God has done so many wonderful things for us and is such a great God! God has so much power, and he uses that power for us.** Ask:

● **How has God's power helped you?**

● **How has God helped you by answering your prayers?**

If kids hesitate to share answers to prayer, tell of a time when God answered one of your prayers. Then return to the classroom.

Say: **We've just spent a few minutes seeing God's works and declaring what good things God has done for us. Now that we have these things in mind, let's spend one minute concentrating on nothing but God. Close your eyes and silently think about God for a minute. I'll let you know when the time is up.**

After one minute, tell the kids to open their eyes. Ask:

● **How hard was it to keep your mind on God? Why?**

● **When is it especially difficult to keep your mind on God?**

Say: **Even though we just saw God's amazing and beautiful creation, we all had trouble keeping our minds focused on God. In our story today, God's people forgot the many miracles God had just done for them. Rather than continuing to thank God, they forgot God and gave in to the temptation to worship an idol.**

2 Picture This

(You'll need Bibles, markers, tape, newsprint, scissors, and photocopies of the "Picture This" handout. Also bring 3×5 cards with one of the following references written on each: Exodus 32:1-6; Exodus 32:7-14; Exodus 32:15-24; and Exodus 32:30-32.)

Form groups of three. Cut apart the "Picture This" handout and give one section to each group. Have the children help you tape the newsprint to the wall, one sheet for each group. Set out markers. Give each group one 3×5 card with a Scripture reference on it. If you have fewer than four groups, form pairs or give each group more than one card. If you have more than four groups, it's OK to give the same Bible passage to more than one group.

Say: **The ancient Egyptians left records in drawings called hieroglyphics. Hieroglyphics are pictures used like words to tell a story. You've probably seen pictures of these writings and drawings in books or magazines. Use the handout I've given you to help you make your own hieroglyphics. Look up and read the Bible passage on your card. On your sheet of newsprint, draw your own hieroglyphics to tell about your part of today's Bible story.**

Allow five minutes for kids to complete the drawings, then have volunteers from each group explain their drawings.

After the students have shared, sit in a circle on the floor and ask:

● **Why did the people want Aaron to make a god for them?**

● **What did they say this calf-idol had done for them?**

● **If you were God, how would this make you feel?**

Say: **The neighboring nations saw how God had delivered the Israelites from Egypt with the parting of the Red Sea.** Ask:

● **When these neighboring nations saw that God's people began to worship idols, what do you think they thought?**

Say: **When God's people saw other nations worshiping idols, they were tempted to worship idols, too. Let's see what can happen when we face temptation.**

3 ► God Cures Temptation's Lures

(You'll need a Bible and an attractive fishing lure. If you don't have one, draw a picture of a fishhook or bend a piece of wire to look like a fishhook.)

Pass the fishing lure around so that each person can feel it. Warn kids about touching the sharp points of the hook.

Say: **Temptation begins in our thoughts. God's people took their minds off the one true God, and this tempted them to do wrong things.** Ask:

● **If a fish could think, what do you think would go through its mind when it first sees a fishing lure in the water?**

● **How is this like when we're tempted to do something wrong?**

● **What kinds of things go through our minds when we're lured into temptation?**

● **What happens to the fish when it takes the bait?**

● **What happens to us when we "take the bait" of temptation?**

Read 1 Corinthians 10:13. Say: **When temptation comes, we can either give in to it or ask ourselves, "What does God want me to do in this situation?" and obey God. God will use his power to help us avoid temptation.**

Form groups of two or three.

Say: **Each group is to think of a situation in which a person your age would be tempted to do something wrong. For example, you're at the pool and you see someone drop a pair of goggles. Because you've been wanting some goggles, you're tempted to pick them up and keep them.**

Then, one group at a time, you will describe your temptation and call on another group to tell how to respond to that temptation the way God wants us to. An example of a response could be "Even though I wanted to keep the goggles, I'd pick them up and give them back to the person who dropped them."

Have each group choose who will share the temptation and who will choose a different group to respond. Give groups two minutes to think of their situations. Then have each group tell its situation and ask for a response from another group. Make sure each group is chosen to respond.

Say: **We all face temptations. Having a temptation is not wrong. It is wrong to yield to the temptation and do wrong things. Let's see what happens when we give in to temptation.**

4 Let Your Light Shine

(You'll need Bibles, birthday candles, aluminum foil, and matches.)

Before class, cover the bottom of each birthday candle with aluminum foil, spreading the foil out to make a small platform for wax to drip on.

Say: **When we turn away from temptation and act according to God's rules, people notice.**

Help kids find Matthew 5:16 in their Bibles. If everyone has the same translation, read the verse in unison. If not, have a volunteer read the verse to the class. Then give each child a candle and turn off the lights. Have the children hold out their candles as you light them with a match. Ask:

● **What happens to a darkened room when candles are lit?**
● **How are we like these candles when we do what is right?**
● **What can you do to shine like a candle in a dark room?**

Tell the children to blow out the candles, then ask:

● **How is blowing out the candles like giving in to temptation?**

Have kids stand in a circle. Relight one child's candle. As you do so, say: (Child's name), **let your light shine!** Have that child light the candle of the person next to him or her and repeat the phrase. Continue until all the candles are re-lit.

Say: **Hold your candles in front of you as we pray. Dear God, give us strength not to give in to temptation. Show us what you want us to do so we can be lights for you in this world. Amen.**

Blow out the candles, and lay them aside.

5 Keep That Flame Burning

(You'll need a city map, tape, and red or yellow construction paper. If you live in a small town, sketch a map of your town, identifying streets on which

91

the kids in your class live. Many phone books also include city maps.)

Give each child a small piece of construction paper. Tell the children to tear out the shape of a small flame. As they do so, tape the city map to a wall.

Say: **When you're finished with your paper flames, find your street on this map and tape your flame to your street. As you tape it, decide one thing you can do to keep your light shining for God in your little corner of the world. For example, you could decide to be kind to your elderly neighbor. Or you might invite someone you usually don't play with to come over. Or you may pick up trash in a nearby park.**

After the flames have been taped, gather kids around the map and ask:

● **How have we changed the map of our city?**

● **How do you think our city would change if everyone who follows God would let his or her light shine for God?**

● **What will you do this week to let your light shine for God?**

As each child mentions something he or she will do this week, encourage the other kids to encourage the child by saying such things as "You can do it!" or "That's a great idea!"

Say: **Let's ask God to help us do what we've decided.**

6 Candy-Corn Prayer

(You'll need candy corn or yellow gumdrops for this activity.)

Have kids sit on the floor in a circle. Give each person a piece of candy.

Say: **This candy reminds me of a candle flame. We'll go around the circle praying. When it's your turn, hold up your candy like a light and say, "God, help me to..." then add what you've decided to do to let your light shine for God. Then eat your candy flame.**

When kids have each had a turn, close by praying: **Thank you, God, for letting us be lights for you. Help us shine our lights this week. Amen.**

Have the children take their flames from the map.

Say: **Take your flame home to help you remember what you have decided to do this week for God.**

PICTURE THIS

WATER   ISLAND   HOUSE   CITY

TO GO   LAKE   DOG   TO GO

COW   WATER   RAM   HOUSE

CITY   CALF   LAKE   DONKEY

LESSON 13

STARS BURSTING WITH TALENT

Story: The People Give Their Talents and Possessions to God's Work
Exodus 35:29–36:7
Good News: God gives us each talents and abilities.

God commanded the Israelites to build a tabernacle so God could dwell among his people. Many people brought gifts out of the abundance God had given them. God gave other people gifts of wisdom, ability, and understanding to do the skilled work needed. As the people combined their possessions and talents, the tabernacle was completed.

Psalm 119:73 says, "You made me and formed me with your hands." Pride makes it easy to believe that what we accomplish is done strictly through our own efforts. Yet the Bible says God is the one who makes us what we are. Use this lesson to teach middle-elementary kids that God gives them individual talents and abilities to use in his service.

A Look at the Lesson

1. One-of-a-Kind Design (10 minutes)—Students will design pictures and talk about their different talents and abilities.

2. Talent on Loan (10 minutes)—Kids will hear a Bible story from Exodus 35:29–36:7 and talk about how God gets his work done on earth.

3. Stars Bursting (15 minutes)—Kids will play a game with Starburst fruit chews, listen to Matthew 25:20-23, and discuss how God increases talents.

4. Full of Talent (15 minutes)—Children will encourage one another to use their talents for God.

5. Play Ball! (7 minutes)—Students will play sports with the wrong equipment, listen to Psalm 119:73, and learn that they've each been made for a specific purpose.

6. Talented Prayer-Circle (3 minutes)—Students will thank God for their talents.

Preparation

Gather Bibles and an assortment of small items such as scraps of construction paper and gift wrap, odd pieces of fabric or fake fur, tissue paper, unusual buttons, old greeting cards, and yarn or string. Also bring paper, glue, glitter, scissors, pencils, Starburst fruit chews, cups, a football, a tennis ball, a Ping-Pong ball, and a garbage can.

1 One-of-a-Kind Design

(Set out an assortment of small items such as scraps of construction paper and gift wrap, odd pieces of fabric or fake fur, tissue paper, unusual buttons, old greeting cards, and yarn or string. Also set out paper, glue, glitter, scissors, and pencils.)

Say: **Design a picture of your creative talents. Use any of the materials on this table. Stretch your imagination, but be sure you can explain what your creation shows about yourself and your talents. For example, if you like to paint, you might cut out a paintbrush from gift wrap and glue glitter "paint splashes" around it. Or if you're good at math, you might cut fabric scraps into shapes such as squares and triangles and construction paper into numbers and** arrange them on your paper. Sign your creation when you finish. You have four minutes.

When time is up, have kids hold up their pictures one at a time and describe what the designs show about themselves. Ask:

● **What made these designs fun to create?**

● **What makes these designs interesting to look at?**

● **How would the pictures have turned out if everyone had used the same items to make the same designs?**

● **What would it be like if everyone on earth had the same likes and dislikes and the same talents and abilities?**

Say: **The world is more interesting and beautiful because God made people different. God created each of us a one-of-a-kind person. He gives us the ability to do special things. In our Bible story today, God's people combine their talents and possessions to build a special place for God.**

Talent on Loan

(You'll need a Bible.)

Form two groups. Say: **You're going to help me teach the lesson. When I point to group 1, say, "God gave." When I point to group 2, say, "the ability." Let's practice for a minute.**

Point to each group a couple of times until kids respond quickly. Open your Bible to Exodus 35.

Say: **Our story today is found in Exodus. God told Moses to build a tabernacle—a holy tent where the people could worship God. God told Moses exactly how to build it. Many people brought offerings to help build the tabernacle. They brought whatever they had: gold, silver, fabrics, jewels, pretty stones, and oil and spices. This was going to be the most beautiful tent ever made!** Ask:

How did God get this tent made? (Point to group 1 and wait for the group to say, "God gave") **a man named Bezalel** (point to group 2 and wait for that group to say, "the ability") **to do artistic work for the holy tent.** (Point to group 1, "God gave") **Bezalel** (point to group 2, "the ability") **to create designs in gold, silver, and bronze.** (Point to group 1, "God gave") **Bezalel** (point to group 2, "the ability") **to cut jewels and carve wood.** (Point to group 1, "God gave") **Bezalel and a man named Oholiab** (point to group 2, "the ability") **to teach their crafts to others.** (Point to group 1, "God gave") **other people** (point to group 2, "the ability") **to sew and weave.**

The Israelites continued to bring their gifts every morning. The people brought so many offerings that soon the workers asked Moses to tell the people to stop bringing their gifts—they had enough for the tabernacle. A command went throughout the camp telling the people to stop bringing their gifts because the workers had more than enough to finish the work. God's beautiful tabernacle would soon be completed because (point to group 1, "God gave") **the people** (point to Group 2, "the ability") **to make it.**

Ask:

● **God wanted a tabernacle for worship. How did God get this tent made?**

● **How does God accomplish things here on earth?**

Say: **God uses our talents and abilities to do his will. In fact, God created us to do good things here on earth. Let's find out more about our special gifts.**

3 Stars Bursting

(You'll need Bibles, cups, and Starburst fruit chews.)

Give each child a cup and six pieces of Starburst fruit chews. Have kids set their cups three or four feet in front of them.

Say: **Let's play a game with fruit chews. Try throwing your fruit chews into your cup. Each time one of your fruit chews lands in your cup, move forward one shoe length.**

When the kids have tossed all their fruit chews, have them retrieve their cups and fruit chews and sit in a circle. Ask:

● **Was it easy or hard to toss your fruit chews into the cup? Why?**

● **Did it get easier as you moved forward? Explain.**

● **Think about the first time you tried to play a video game or ride a bike. What happened?**

● **What did you do to get better at it?**

Say: **As you tossed your fruit chews, I allowed you to move closer for each piece that landed inside your cup. That made it easier for you to toss the next piece. When we use the talents and abilities God gives us, they become easier for us. People aren't born with the ability to play a complicated song on the piano or to play a sport. God gives us the talent and the desire to do something. As we practice our gifts, we become good at them.**

Jesus told a story about two men who used their talents for God. Let's read what happened. Have volunteers read Matthew 25:20-23. Ask:

● **These servants knew how to invest money. What happened** when the servants used their money wisely?

● **What happens when we use our gifts wisely?**

● **What do these verses say God will do for us if we make good use of the talents God has given us?**

● **What would it be like to have even more talents and abilities than you have now?**

Say: **As we faithfully use the talents and abilities God has already given us, he will give us more and more opportunities to use what we have. The Bible says God will increase our talents. These fruit chews are called Starbursts. With God's help, each of us will become stars bursting with talent for God! Let's each eat a Starburst to celebrate God's good gifts to us.**

Have everyone eat one Starburst. Then have kids put the rest of their fruit chews aside to take home. Gather the cups and set them aside for use in the "Play Ball!" activity.

(You'll need the designs the kids made in the first activity.)

Have kids get their "One-of-a-Kind" designs and sit in a circle.

Say: **The designs you made earlier represent talents or abilities God has given you. Let's think about ways we could use these talents for God.**

Have one person at a time stand in the middle of the circle while the other kids brainstorm ways that person could use the talent to serve God. For example, if a child chose reading as a talent, he or she could read to a sick friend or volunteer to read to the children in the church nursery. Then have kids encourage that person with statements such as "You're a good reader" or "You'll do a good job of reading to little kids."

Say: **This class is so full of talented people. Isn't it great that God has given you such wonderful abilities! But sometimes we start looking at what God has given someone else and wish we had that talent instead. Let me show you something that might help if you ever start feeling that way.**

5 Play Ball!

(You'll need a Bible, a football, a tennis ball, and a Ping-Pong ball. You'll also need an empty garbage can and the cups used in the "Stars Bursting" activity.)

Set the garbage can on one side of the room, two chairs next to each other on the other side, and the cups in the middle of the room. Send kids who want to play basketball to the garbage can. Send those who want to play volleyball to the chairs. Explain that the chairs are to be used as a net. Tell those who want to bowl to gather around the cups. If you have fewer than 10 kids, set up only the basketball and volleyball areas.

Give the football to the basketball players, the tennis ball to the volleyball players, and the Ping-Pong ball to the bowlers.

Say: **Try playing your sport with the balls I've given you. If you get frustrated, you may switch to another sport.**

After three minutes, call time. Gather kids in a circle. Ask:

● **What was it like trying to play a sport using the wrong equipment?**

● **How is playing a sport using the wrong equipment like expecting to be good at someone else's talent?**

Read Psalm 119:73.

● **How does knowing that God made you special help you be satisfied with the talents and gifts God has given you?**

● **How does knowing God's commands help us use our talents for God's service?**

Say: **Just as each of these balls works very well when it's used with the proper sport, God has given us varied abilities to be used at different times for his service. Your talent is just as important as the talent of the person sitting next to you. When you start comparing yourself to others or feeling jealous of what God has given someone else, it helps to thank God for what he has given you. Let's thank God right now for our talents.**

6 Talented Prayer-Circle

(You'll need the "One-of-a-Kind" designs the kids made earlier.)

Form a circle. Have each child hold up his or her design and, in a sentence, thank God for his or her talent. Close with the following prayer: **God, just as each of the balls we used earlier is of great use in its own sport, we, too, have our own special and unique talents from you. Let**

us be thankful for what you have given us. Help us gladly use our talents for your service. Amen.

Have kids take their "One-of-a-Kind" designs home as reminders to use their abilities for God in the upcoming week.